Index of Biblical Images

Other titles by Warren W. Wiersbe (selected)

Being a Child of God
Be Myself
The Bible Exposition Commentary (2 vols.)
The Bumps Are What You Climb On
The Cross of Jesus: What His Words from Calvary Mean for Us
Developing a Christian Imagination
Elements of Preaching
God Isn't in a Hurry: Learning to Slow Down and Live
The Intercessory Prayer of Jesus: Priorities for Dynamic Christian Living
Living with the Giants: The Lives of Great Men of the Faith
Meet Yourself in the Psalms
The Names of Jesus
On Being a Servant of God
Prayer, Praise, and Promises: A Daily Walk through the Psalms
Run with the Winners
So That's What a Christian Is! 12 Pictures of the Dynamic Christian Life
The Strategy of Satan
Turning Mountains into Molehills: And Other Devotional Talks
Victorious Christians You Should Know
Wiersbe's Expository Outlines on the New Testament
Wiersbe's Expository Outlines on the Old Testament
Windows on the Parables

Index of Biblical Images

Similes, Metaphors, and Symbols in Scripture

Based on the text of *The New International Version* of the Bible

Warren W. Wiersbe

A Division of Baker Book House Co
Grand Rapids, Michigan 49516

Published by Baker Books
a division of Baker Book House Company
P.O. Box 6287, Grand Rapids, MI 49516-6287

Printed in the United States of America

ISBN 0-8010-9107-1

Library of Congress Cataloging-in-Publication Data is on file at the Library of Congress, Washington, D.C.

For information about academic books, resources for Christian leaders, and all new releases available from Baker Book House, visit our web site:
http://www.bakerbooks.com

Contents

Preface

"The great teacher is the one who turns our ears into eyes so that we can see the truth."

That eastern proverb helps us better understand why the Bible is a "picture book" and the Holy Spirit chose to share the truth of God through metaphorical language. No matter where you turn in Scripture, you find historians, prophets, poets, apostles, and especially our Lord Jesus Christ teaching eternal truth by means of picture language. To ignore the imagery of Scripture is to misread God's Word and ultimately to misinterpret it.

It's been my privilege to teach a Doctor of Ministry course for several seminaries on "imagination and biblical preaching." Our basic text was my book *Preaching and Teaching with Imagination* (Baker Book House), but both the students and I often wished for an index of biblical images to help us locate verses using the same image. The *Dictionary of Biblical Imagery,* edited by Leland Ryken, James C. Wilhoit, and Tremper Longman III (InterVarsity, 1998), hadn't been published yet; in fact, it appeared too late for me to use it in preparing this book. It is a superb work and ought to be used by everyone who wants to teach or preach the Word of God accurately and effectively.

The purpose of this *Index of Biblical Images* is to assist the serious student of Scripture to locate and compare verses from the Bible that use the same or similar imagery in conveying God's truth. For example, you can look up "light" and find what the image means in different contexts. In so doing, you may discover meanings that you have missed in the past.

When a compilation of this nature and size is the work of one author, there are bound to be errors and omissions, and I would appreciate concerned readers telling me about them.

Appreciate the fact that I have frequently had to wrestle with contradictory interpretations and even the question of whether or not a statement is metaphorical, and I have simply had to make judgment calls to the best of my ability. Matters of eschatology have often entered in, and not every user will always agree with my conclusions. I hope, however, that these minor differences will not keep the student from benefiting from using this book.

As Dr. Samuel Johnson wrote in the preface to his *Dictionary of the English Language,* "In this work, when it shall be found that much is omitted, let it not be forgotten that much likewise is performed." If this book encourages others who are more capable to give us a better tool for identifying and classifying biblical images, then these years of labor have not been in vain.

I want to thank our son Bob Wiersbe for assisting me with the computer work. He is in no way responsible for the book's defects but deserves a large share of the credit for its existence! Also a special thank you to my wife, Betty, who assisted in checking the proofs. She turned a toilsome task into an adventure.

Warren W. Wiersbe

A

Account/ Impute

Answer for One's Actions

Gen. 9:5
Gen. 42:22
Deut. 18:19
Josh. 22:23
2 Chron. 24:22
Job 31:14
Job 31:37
Ps. 10:13
Ps. 10:15
Eccles. 3:15
Ezek. 3:18
Ezek. 3:20
Ezek. 33:6
Ezek. 33:8
Ezek. 34:10
Jonah 1:14

An Oath of Judgment

1 Sam. 20:16

Keep a Record (of Sin)

1 Cor. 13:5

Put to One's Credit/Impute

Gen. 15:6
Ps. 106:31
Ezek. 18:20
Rom. 4:3–11
Rom. 4:22
Rom. 4:24
Rom. 6:11
2 Cor. 5:19
Gal. 3:6

Evaluate

Luke 22:37
Rom. 8:18
Rom. 8:36
Rom. 14:14
1 Cor. 4:1
2 Cor. 12:6
Phil. 3:13
Heb. 11:19

Adam

Gen. 2:20

A Type of Christ

Rom. 5:12–21
1 Cor. 15:20–22
1 Cor. 15:45–49

Adultery

(see also Prostitute/ Prostitution)

Worldliness

James 4:4
Rev. 14:8
Rev. 17:2
Rev. 17:4
Rev. 18:3
Rev. 18:9
Rev. 19:2

Idolatry

Jer. 3:8
Jer. 3:20
Jer. 5:7
Jer. 7:9
Jer. 9:2
Jer. 13:27
Jer. 23:14
Ezek. 6:9
Ezek. 16:32
Ezek. 16:38
Ezek. 23:37
Ezek. 23:43
Ezek. 23:45
Hosea 1:2
Hosea 2:2
Hosea 2:4
Hosea 3:1
Hosea 4:2
Hosea 4:13–15
Hosea 7:4

Alien

(see also Stranger)

God as an Alien

Jer. 14:8

The Transiency of Life

1 Chron. 29:15
Ps. 39:12
Ps. 119:19

Gentiles (Outside the Covenant)

Eph. 2:19

The Church

1 Peter 2:11

The Patriarchs

Gen. 17:8
Gen. 21:23
Gen. 23:4
Gen. 28:4
Gen. 47:9
Ps. 105:23
Heb. 11:8–16

Israel

Lev. 25:23
Ps. 105:12

Christ

Ps. 69:8
John 7:5

Anchor

Hope in Christ

Heb. 6:18

Apple/Apple of His Eye/Apple Tree

That Which Is Precious

Deut. 32:10
Ps. 17:8
Prov. 7:2
Zech. 2:8

A Lover

Song of Sol. 2:3

Apt Words

Prov. 25:11

Fragrant Breath

Song of Sol. 7:8

Archer

Hiring a Fool

Prov. 26:10

Ark (Noah)

Salvation

1 Peter 3:20

Arm

Victory

Ezek. 30:24

Defeat

Ps. 10:15
Ezek. 30:21–22

God's Power

Exod. 6:6
Exod. 15:16
Num. 11:23
Deut. 4:34
Deut. 5:15
Deut. 7:19
Deut. 9:29
Deut. 11:2
Deut. 26:8
Deut. 33:27
1 Kings 8:42
2 Kings 17:36
2 Chron. 6:32
Job 40:9
Ps. 44:3
Ps. 77:15
Ps. 89:10
Ps. 89:13
Ps. 89:21
Ps. 98:1
Ps. 136:12
Isa. 30:30
Isa. 30:32
Isa. 50:2
Isa. 51:5
Isa. 51:9
Isa. 52:10
Isa. 59:1
Isa. 59:16
Isa. 62:8
Isa. 63:5
Isa. 63:12
Jer. 21:5
Jer. 27:5
Jer. 32:17
Jer. 32:21
Ezek. 20:33–34
Luke 1:51
John 12:38

God's Salvation/Savior

Isa. 40:11
Isa. 53:1

Attitude of Faith

1 Peter 4:1

Arms/Armor

Christian Graces

1 Thess. 5:8

Spiritual Equipment for Warfare

Isa. 59:17
Eph. 6:14–18

Army

(see also Warfare)

God's Terrors

Job 6:4

Job 10:17
Job 19:12

Life (Difficult)

Job 7:1
Job 14:14
Isa. 40:2

God

Job 15:33

Challenges

2 Sam. 22:30
Ps. 18:29

Majesty/Glory

Song of Sol. 6:4

Aroma

(see Fragrance/ Incense)

Arrow

Lies

Prov. 25:18
Prov. 26:18–19
Jer. 9:8

God's Judgment

Deut. 32:42
Ps. 120:4
Zech. 9:14

God's Discipline

Job 6:4
Ps. 38:2

Evil Words

Ps. 57:4
Ps. 64:3–4

Defeat (Blunted Arrows)

Ps. 58:7

Lightning

Ps. 18:14
Ps. 77:17
Ps. 144:6

Sons

Ps. 127:4

Deliverance

2 Kings 13:18–19

Ashes

Shame

2 Sam. 13:19
Job 30:19

Humility/Repentance

Gen. 18:27
Esther 4:1
Esther 4:3
Job 2:8
Job 42:6
Jer. 6:26
Ezek. 27:30
Dan. 9:3
Matt. 11:21
Luke 10:13

Uselessness/Vanity

Job 13:12
Isa. 44:20

Sorrow/Pain

Ps. 102:9

Frost

Ps. 147:16

Defeat

Mal. 4:3

Athletics

(see also Run/Runner/ Race)

Discipline

1 Tim. 4:7–8
1 Cor. 9:25–27
Heb. 5:14

Faithfulness

Acts 20:24
Gal. 2:2
Gal. 5:7
Phil. 2:16
Phil. 3:12
Phil. 3:15
2 Tim. 4:7–8

Suffering

1 Cor. 4:9
1 Tim. 6:12

Teamwork (Unity)

Phil. 1:27–30
Phil. 4:3

Determination

Phil. 3:12–15
Col. 1:29
Col. 2:1
Heb. 12:1–2

Obedience

2 Tim. 2:5

Awaking

God Begins to Work

Ps. 7:6
Ps. 35:23
Ps. 44:23
Ps. 73:20
Ps. 78:65
Ps. 80:2
Isa. 51:9

Preparation to Act/Alertness

Isa. 51:17
Isa. 52:1
Rom. 13:11
Eph. 5:14
Rev. 3:2–3
Rev. 16:15

Resurrection

Ps. 139:18
Isa. 26:19
Dan. 12:2
John 11:11
1 Thess. 5:10

Ax

Divine Judgment

Isa. 10:34
Jer. 46:22
Matt. 3:10
Luke 3:9

Human Destructiveness

Ps. 74:5–6

Overcoming Handicaps

Eccles. 10:10

Pride

Isa. 10:15

B

Babel/Babylon

Confusion

Gen. 11:9

Rebellion (Anti-God World System)

Rev. 14:8
Rev. 16:19
Rev. 18:1–3

Apostate Religion

Rev. 17:1–6

Rome (?)

1 Peter 5:13

Images of the Babylonian Empire

Jewel

Isa. 13:19

Gold Cup

Jer. 51:7

Threshing Floor

Jer. 51:33

Mother of Prostitutes

Rev. 17:5

War Club

Jer. 51:20

Mountain

Jer. 51:25

Hammer

Jer. 50:23

Bandit

Sudden Poverty

Prov. 6:11
Prov. 24:33

A Prostitute

Prov. 23:28

Banner

God's Help

Ps. 20:5
Ps. 60:4
Isa. 11:12
Isa. 18:3
Isa. 49:22
Isa. 62:10

God's Judgment

Isa. 5:26
Isa. 13:2
Isa. 30:17
Jer. 50:2
Jer. 51:12
Jer. 51:27

Messiah

Isa. 11:10

Love

Song of Sol. 2:4

Majesty

Song of Sol. 6:4

Barrenness/ Barren Woman

Israel

Isa. 49:21
Isa. 54:1
Gal. 4:27

Restoration

Isa. 41:18

Bed

Ungodliness

Isa. 28:20

Sexual Sin

Deut. 22:30
Deut. 27:20
1 Chron. 5:1
Ezek. 22:10

Laziness

Prov. 26:14

Idolatry

Isa. 57:7–8
Ezek. 23:17

Suffering/Judgment

Rev. 2:22

Bees

Enemies/Invasion

Deut. 1:44
Ps. 118:12
Isa. 7:18

Belt

Cursing

Ps. 109:18–19

Israel

Jer. 13:1–11

Righteousness

Isa. 11:5

Suffering

Acts 21:11

Truth

Eph. 6:14

Readiness

Exod. 12:11
1 Kings 18:46
2 Kings 4:29
2 Kings 9:1
Isa. 5:27

Bind/Bound

Close Relationship

Gen. 44:30
1 Sam. 18:1
1 Sam. 25:29

Obligation (Oath)

Josh. 2:17
1 Sam. 14:24
1 Sam. 14:27–29
Neh. 9:38
Neh. 10:29
Isa. 56:6
Jer. 50:5
Matt. 23:16
Matt. 23:18
Acts 23:12

Suffering

Job 16:8
Job 30:18

Sin

Lam. 1:14

Sin Unforgiven

Matt. 16:19
Matt. 18:18

Salvation

Ps. 147:3
Isa. 30:26
Isa. 61:1
Ezek. 34:16
Hosea 6:1

Satanic Bondage

Luke 13:16

Marriage

Rom. 7:2
1 Cor. 7:15
1 Cor. 7:39

Judgment

Jude 1:6
Rev. 20:2

Obedience (to God)

Prov. 3:3
Prov. 6:20–21
Prov. 7:2–3

Unity/Love

Col. 3:14

Birds

(see also Eagle)

God

Exod. 19:4
Deut. 32:11–12

The Holy Spirit

Gen. 1:2
John 1:32–33

Satan

Matt. 13:4
Matt. 13:19

Angelic Creatures

Ezek. 1:10
Dan. 7:6
Rev. 4:7

Renewal

Ps. 103:5
Isa. 40:31

Deliverance

Exod. 19:4
Ps. 124:7
Prov. 6:5
Rev. 12:14

Being Trapped/Snared

Prov. 7:23
Eccles. 9:12
Lam. 3:52
Ezek. 13:20

Escape/Fleeing

Ps. 11:1
Isa. 16:2
Jer. 48:28

Pride

Jer. 49:16
Obad. 1:4
Hab. 2:9

Judgment/Invasion

Isa. 10:14
Isa. 46:11
Jer. 12:9
Jer. 48:40
Jer. 49:22
Ezek. 17:3
Ezek. 17:7
Hosea 8:1

Swiftness

2 Sam. 1:23
Jer. 4:13

Deception

Jer. 5:27

Foolishness

Hosea 7:12
Hosea 11:11

Loneliness

Ps. 102:7

Insecurity

Prov. 23:5
Prov. 27:8
Hosea 9:11

Birth

(see also Pregnancy/ Conception/Birth, Travail [in Birth])

Disgrace/Failure

2 Kings 19:3
Isa. 37:3
Hosea 9:11

Despair/Futility

Num. 11:12
Job 3:1
Job 3:3
Job 3:11
Job 5:7
Isa. 26:18
Isa. 33:11
Jer. 15:10
Jer. 20:14

Resurrection/ Restoration

Isa. 26:19
Isa. 66:7

Temptation/Sin

Job 15:35
Ps. 7:14
Isa. 59:4
James 1:15

Salvation

John 1:13
John 3:1
1 Cor. 15:8
James 1:18
1 Peter 1:3
1 Peter 1:23
1 John 2:29
1 John 3:9
1 John 4:7
1 John 5:1
1 John 5:4
1 John 5:18

The Impossible

Job 11:12
Isa. 66:8

Creation

Job 15:7
Job 38:8
Job 38:28–29
Ps. 90:2

Bit

(see Reins/Bit/Bridle)

Blemishes

(see also Blots/Blot Out)

False Teachers

2 Peter 2:13
Jude 1:12

Defilements in the Church

Eph. 5:27

Blind, Blindness

False Teachers

Matt. 15:14
Matt. 23:16–17
Matt. 23:19
Matt. 23:24
Matt. 23:26
Luke 6:39
John 9:39–40

Religious Stupor/Spiritually Ignorant

Isa. 29:9
Isa. 42:7
Isa. 42:16
Isa. 42:18–19
Isa. 43:8
Isa. 56:10
2 Cor. 4:4
Rev. 3:17

Spiritual Pride

Rom. 2:19

Rejection of Truth

2 Peter 1:9

Blood

Vengeance

Gen. 4:10
2 Sam. 21:1
Job 16:18
Isa. 26:21
Rev. 6:10

Grace (Blood Speaking)

Heb. 12:24

Guilt/ Accountability (Hands/Head Stained)

Lev. 20:9
Lev. 20:11–13
Lev. 20:16
Lev. 20:27
Josh. 2:19
2 Sam. 1:16
2 Sam. 3:29
2 Sam. 4:11
1 Kings 2:33
1 Kings 2:37
Isa. 1:15
Isa. 59:3
Ezek. 3:18
Ezek. 3:20
Ezek. 18:13
Ezek. 33:4–8
Matt. 23:35
Luke 11:50
Acts 1:19
Acts 5:28
Acts 18:6
Acts 20:26

Circumcision

Exod. 4:24–26

Impending Judgment

Exod. 12:7
Exod. 12:13
Exod. 12:22–23

Life

Lev. 17:11
Deut. 12:23
2 Sam. 23:17
1 Chron. 11:19

Slaughter

Deut. 32:42
Ps. 58:10
Ps. 68:23
Isa. 34:6
Isa. 49:26
Jer. 46:10
Ezek. 39:19
Rev. 16:6
Rev. 17:6

Agony

Luke 22:44

Receiving Eternal Life (Drinking)

John 6:53–56

The Atoning Death of Christ

Rev. 12:11

Grape Juice

Gen. 49:11

Blots/Blot Out

Judgment

Exod. 17:14
Exod. 32:32–33
Deut. 9:14
Deut. 25:19
Deut. 29:20
Deut. 32:26
2 Kings 14:27
Neh. 4:5
Neh. 13:14
Ps. 9:5
Ps. 69:28
Ps. 109:13–14
Jer. 18:23
Rev. 3:5

Forgiveness

Ps. 51:1
Ps. 51:9
Ps. 109:14
Neh. 4:5
Isa. 43:25
Jer. 18:23

Death

Exod. 32:32–33
Ps. 69:28
Rev. 3:5

Loss of Reward

Neh. 13:14

False Teachers

2 Peter 2:13

End of a Family Name

Deut. 25:6
Ps. 109:13

Boat/Ship/Shipwreck

Swiftness of Life

Job 9:26

A Faithful Wife

Prov. 31:14

Apostasy

1 Tim. 1:19

Tyre ("Ship of State")

Ezek. 27:1–9
Ezek. 27:25–30

Bones

House of Israel

Ezek. 37:11

Decayed Bones

Disgraceful Wife

Prov. 12:4

Envy

Prov. 14:30

Awe

Hab. 3:13

Burning Bones

Suffering

Ps. 102:3
Lam. 1:13

Strong Desire

Jer. 20:9

Broken Bones

Chastening

Ps. 51:8
Lam. 3:4

Exploitation

Micah 3:2–3

Bow

(see also Arrow)

Fresh Vigor

Job 29:20

Suffering (Unstrung)

Job 30:11

Divine Judgment (Bent Bow)

Ps. 7:12
Ps. 21:12
Lam. 2:4
Lam. 3:12
Hab. 3:9

Victory (Broken Bow)

1 Sam. 2:4
Ps. 37:15
Ps. 46:9
Jer. 49:35
Jer. 51:56
Ezek. 39:3
Hosea 1:5
Hab. 3:9
Zech. 9:10

Undependability (Faulty Bow)

Ps. 78:57
Hosea 7:16

Dependability

Gen. 49:24

The Tongue (Words as Weapons)

Ps. 11:2
Ps. 64:3–4
Prov. 26:18–19
Jer. 9:3
Jer. 9:8
Jer. 18:18

God's People (God's Weapons)

Zech. 9:13

Strength

Ps. 18:34

Branch

(see also Vine)

Rejection

Isa. 14:19
Jer. 5:10
John 15:2
John 15:6

Messiah/Jesus

Isa. 4:2
Isa. 11:1
Jer. 23:5
Jer. 33:15
Zech. 3:8
Zech. 6:12

Prosperity

Job 15:32
Job 29:19

Judgment

Job 18:16
Jer. 11:16
Jer. 48:32
Ezek. 19:12
Ezek. 19:14
Ezek. 31:1–13

Israel (Vine)

Ps. 80:10
Ezek. 17:6–8
Ezek. 17:23
Ezek. 19:10–14

God's Servants

Zech. 4:12

Believers

John 15:1–6
Rom. 11:16–24

Bread

Christ

John 6:32–35
John 6:41
John 6:48
John 6:58

The Body of Christ

Matt. 26:26
Mark 14:22
Luke 22:19
John 6:51
1 Cor. 10:16–17
1 Cor. 11:23–24

Sorrow/Discipline (Bread and Water)

Deut. 16:3
1 Kings 22:27
2 Chron. 18:26
Ps. 80:5
Isa. 30:20

Vanity (What Is Not Bread)

Isa. 55:2

Sincerity/Truth (Unleavened)

1 Cor. 5:8

Promised Victory

Judg. 7:13–14

Poverty

1 Sam. 2:36
Ps. 37:25
Prov. 6:26

Exploiting People

Ps. 14:4
Ps. 53:4

Friendship (Share Bread)

Ps. 41:9
Obad. 1:7
Mark 14:20
John 13:18
John 13:26

Sin (Eat Bread of Wickedness)

Prov. 4:17
Prov. 28:21

Idleness

Prov. 31:27

Industriousness

Eccles. 11:1

The Word of God

Deut. 8:3
Job 23:12
Matt. 4:4
Luke 4:4

Breath

(see also Wind/Whirlwind)

Life

Gen. 1:30
Gen. 2:7
Gen. 6:17
Gen. 7:15
Gen. 7:22
Job 12:10
Job 27:3
Job 33:4
Job 34:14–15
Isa. 2:22
Isa. 42:5
Isa. 57:16
Jer. 38:16
Ezek. 37:5–10
Acts 17:25

God's Wrath

Exod. 15:10
2 Sam. 22:16
Job 4:9
Job 15:30
Ps. 18:15
Isa. 11:4
Isa. 30:28
Isa. 30:33
Isa. 40:7
Isa. 59:19
Ezek. 21:31
2 Thess. 2:8

God's Creative Power

Job 26:13
Job 37:10
Ps. 33:6

The Holy Spirit

Job 32:8
Ezek. 37:5–10
John 3:8
John 20:22

The Sinner's Self-Destruction

Isa. 33:11

Brevity of Life

Job 7:7
Ps. 39:5
Ps. 39:11
Ps. 62:9
Ps. 144:4

Wrath of Man

Ps. 27:12
Isa. 25:4
Acts 9:1

Death (Breathe Your Last)

Gen. 25:8
Gen. 25:17
Gen. 35:18
Gen. 35:29
Gen. 49:33
Job 14:10
Mark 15:37
Luke 23:46

Bride

Israel

Isa. 49:18
Isa. 61:10
Jer. 2:2
Jer. 2:32
Hosea 1:2
Hosea 3:1

The Church

John 3:29
2 Cor. 11:2
Eph. 5:22–32

Rev. 19:7
Rev. 21:2

The Holy City

Rev. 21:9

Bridegroom

Israel

Isa. 61:10

Rejoicing

Isa. 62:5

The Sun

Ps. 19:5

Christ

Matt. 9:15
Mark 2:19–20
Luke 5:34–35
John 3:29
2 Cor. 11:2–3

Bridle

(see Reins/Bit/Bridle)

Broom

(see Sweep [Away])

Bruises/Wounds

National Decay/Defeat

Isa. 1:5
Jer. 6:7
Jer. 6:14
Jer. 8:11
Jer. 8:22
Jer. 14:17
Jer. 30:12
Jer. 30:15
Jer. 30:17
Lam. 2:13
Micah 1:9
Nah. 3:19

Gentleness, Patience

Isa. 42:3
Matt. 12:20

God's Care/Forgiveness

Isa. 30:26
Jer. 30:17
Hosea 6:1

Personal Burden

Ps. 109:22
Jer. 10:19
Jer. 15:18

Injure One's Conscience

1 Cor. 8:12

Hungry Children

Lam. 2:12

Pharaoh

Ezek. 30:24

A Fool

Prov. 26:10

Friendly Counsel

Prov. 27:6

The Atonement

Isa. 53:5
1 Peter 2:24

Building/Builders

The Church

Matt. 16:18
1 Cor. 3:9–10
Eph. 2:20–22
1 Peter 2:5

Evangelism

Rom. 15:20

The Family (Build a House)

Gen. 16:2
Gen. 30:3
Deut. 25:9
2 Sam. 7:27
1 Kings 11:38
1 Chron. 17:10
1 Chron. 17:12
1 Chron. 17:25
Ps. 127:1
Prov. 14:1
Prov. 24:3
Heb. 3:3–4

Leaders as Builders

Ps. 118:22
Matt. 21:42
Mark 12:10
Luke 20:17
Acts 4:11
1 Cor. 3:10
1 Cor. 3:12
1 Peter 2:7

Glorified Body

2 Cor. 5:1

Obeying God's Word

Matt. 7:24–27
Luke 6:48–49

Pride/False Security

Job 39:27
Ps. 78:69
Jer. 49:16

Spiritual Growth (Edify)

Acts 20:32
Rom. 14:19
Rom. 15:2

1 Cor. 8:1
1 Cor. 14:4–5
1 Cor. 14:12
1 Cor. 14:17
2 Cor. 10:8
2 Cor. 13:10
Eph. 4:12
Eph. 4:16
Eph. 4:29
Col. 2:7
1 Thess. 5:11
Jude 1:20

Bulls

(see also Calves, Cows/Heifer)

Tribe of Joseph

Deut. 33:17

Leaders

Isa. 34:7

Enemies

Ps. 22:12
Ps. 68:30

Burden

Guilt

1 Sam. 25:31
Ps. 38:4

Responsibility

Exod. 18:18
Num. 11:11
Num. 11:14
Num. 11:17
Deut. 1:9
Luke 11:46
Acts 15:8
Gal. 6:2
Rev. 2:24

Taxes

Neh. 5:15

Suffering

Job 7:20
Ps. 66:11

Life

Eccles. 1:13
Eccles. 3:10

Hypocrisy

Isa. 1:14
Isa. 43:24

Victory (Burden Removed)

Isa. 10:27
Isa. 14:25

The Law

Gal. 5:1

Bush

The Unbeliever

Jer. 17:5–6

Desertion/Loneliness

Jer. 48:6

Butter

Smooth Speech

Ps. 55:21

C

Calves

(see also Bulls, Cows/Heifer)

Joy

Ps. 29:6
Mal. 4:2

Discipline

Jer. 31:18

Leaders

Isa. 34:7

Soldiers

Jer. 46:21

Enemies

Ps. 68:30

Cake

Compromise/ Insincerity

Hosea 7:8

Camel

Lusting after Sin

Jer. 2:23

Impossibility

Matt. 19:24
Mark 10:25
Luke 18:25

Hypocrisy

Matt. 23:24

Camp

Disgrace (Outside the Camp)

Lev. 24:14
Lev. 24:23
Num. 12:14–15
Heb. 13:13

Separation/Isolation

Lev. 13:46
Lev. 14:3
Lev. 16:27
Num. 5:2–4
Num. 12:14–15
Num. 31:19
Deut. 23:10

Safety

Josh. 6:23

Cart

God's Judgment

Amos 2:13

God's Blessing

Ps. 65:11

Cattle

Stupid People

Job 18:3

God's Guidance

Isa. 63:14

Judgment

Dan. 4:25
Dan. 4:32–33
Dan. 5:21

Cedar

King of Israel (Jehoash)

2 Kings 14:9–10
2 Chron. 25:18–19

The Godly

Ps. 92:12

David's Dynasty

Ezek. 17:1–3

Christ

Ezek. 17:22–23

Assyria

Ezek. 31:3

Spiritual Renewal

Hosea 14:5–6

Israel

Num. 24:6

Chaff

Victim of Circumstances

Job 13:25
Job 21:18

The Insignificant

Job 41:28

The Ungodly (Individuals, Nations)

Job 21:18
Ps. 1:4
Ps. 35:5
Ps. 83:13
Isa. 17:13
Isa. 29:5
Isa. 33:11
Jer. 13:24
Dan. 2:35
Hosea 13:3
Matt. 3:12
Luke 3:17

Princes/Rulers

Isa. 40:24

Conquest

Isa. 41:2
Isa. 41:15

Judgment

Zeph. 2:2

Chains

(see also Bind/Bound)

Parental Instruction

Prov. 1:9

God's Law

Ps. 2:3

An Evil Woman's Hands

Eccles. 7:26

Injustice

Isa. 58:6

Divine Discipline

Isa. 28:22
Lam. 3:7

Eternal Punishment

Jude 1:6

Death

Ps. 116:16

Champion

The Sun

Ps. 19:5

Chariots

Godly Persons

2 Kings 2:12
2 Kings 13:14

False Confidence

Ps. 20:7
Isa. 31:1
Isa. 36:9

God's Might

Ps. 68:17

Locusts

Joel 2:5

Clouds

Ps. 104:3

Child/Children

Judgment (Stillborn)

Ps. 58:8

Humility

Ps. 131:2
Matt. 18:1–3
Mark 9:36
Mark 10:15
Luke 9:46–48
Luke 18:17

Images of Children

Heritage/Reward

Ps. 127:3

Arrows

Ps. 127:4

Plants

Ps. 144:12

Pillars

Ps. 144:12

Crowns

Prov. 17:6

Churning

Anger

Prov. 30:33

Circumcision

Designation for the Jewish People

Acts 10:45
Acts 11:2
Rom. 3:30
Gal. 2:8–9
Col. 4:11
Titus 1:10

Spiritual Change Within

Lev. 26:41
Deut. 10:16
Deut. 30:6
Jer. 4:4
Rom. 2:28–29

Phil. 3:3
Col. 2:11

Cistern

Security

2 Kings 18:31
Isa. 36:16

Faithful Love

Prov. 5:15

Apostasy (Idolatry)

Jer. 2:13

City

God's Servant

Jer. 1:18

Self-Control

Prov. 16:32
Prov. 25:28

Wealth

Prov. 18:11

Believers

Matt. 5:14

God's Covenants

Gal. 4:24–27

Clap (Hands)

Joy of Creation

Ps. 98:8
Isa. 55:12

Joy of God's People

2 Kings 11:12
Ps. 47:1

Arrogance and the Proud

Job 34:37
Lam. 2:15
Ezek. 25:6
Nahum 3:19

God's Terrors (Judgment)

Job 27:23
Ezek. 21:14
Ezek. 22:13

Clay

(see also Potsherd/Pottery [Broken], Potter)

Persons (Body of Clay)

Job 4:19
Job 10:9
Job 33:6
Isa. 64:8
Rom. 9:21
2 Cor. 4:7
2 Tim. 2:20

False Defenses

Job 13:12

Wealth (Clothing)

Job 27:16

Sunrise

Job 38:14

Nations

Jer. 18:6

Devaluation

Lam. 4:2

Weakness

Dan. 2:33–35
Dan. 2:41–45

Cloak

(see also Clothing)

Divine Call

1 Kings 19:19

Cursing

Ps. 109:19

Shame

Ps. 109:29

Zeal

Isa. 59:17

Cloth

Uncleanness

Isa. 30:22

Clothing

(see also Nakedness)

Forgiveness

Gen. 3:21
Zech. 3:1–5

Spiritual Graces

Joy

Ps. 30:11
Ps. 65:12

Strength

Isa. 51:9
Isa. 52:1

Humility

1 Peter 5:5

Compassion

Col. 3:12

The New Self

Eph. 4:24

Beauty and Care of Nature

Matt. 6:30
Luke 12:28

A Covering for Sin

Gen. 9:20–23
Prov. 10:12
1 Peter 4:8

The Glorified Body

1 Cor. 15:53–54
2 Cor. 5:2–4

God's Splendor

Ps. 45:3
Ps. 104:1
Zech. 6:13

Poverty

Deut. 28:47–48
Rev. 3:17–18
Rev. 16:15

Salvation

2 Chron. 6:41
Ps. 132:16
Isa. 61:10

Shame

Job 8:22
Ps. 35:26
Ps. 109:29
Ps. 132:18

Jesus Christ

Rom. 13:14
Gal. 3:27

Darkness

Isa. 50:3

Violence

Ps. 73:6

Light

Ps. 104:2

New Creation

Ps. 102:26

Righteousness

Job 29:14
Ps. 132:9
Rev. 3:4

Mourning

Gen. 37:34
1 Chron. 21:16

Sickness

Job 7:5

Terror

Ezek. 7:18
Ezek. 26:16

Despair

Ezek. 7:27

Conquest

Jer. 43:12

Gloom

Ezek. 31:15

A New Beginning (Change/Wash Clothes)

Gen. 35:2
Gen. 41:14
Gen. 45:22
Exod. 19:10
Exod. 19:14
Lev. 14:8–9
Jer. 52:33
Rev. 3:18

Clouds

Groups of People

Isa. 60:8
1 Thess. 4:17
Heb. 12:1

Glory of God

1 Kings 8:10
2 Chron. 5:13
Ezek. 10:3–4

God's Dwelling

1 Kings 8:12
2 Chron. 6:1
Ps. 97:2

God's Swift Action/Arrival

Deut. 33:26
2 Sam. 22:10–12
Ps. 18:9–11
Ps. 68:4
Ps. 104:3
Nahum 1:3
Matt. 24:30
Matt. 26:64
Mark 13:26
Mark 14:62
Rev. 1:7

Brevity of Life/Death

Job 7:9

Insecurity

Job 30:15

An Invading Army

Isa. 14:31

Impending Judgment

Isa. 18:4

Forgiveness

Isa. 44:22

Earth's Garment

Job 38:9

God's Rejection of Prayers

Lam. 3:44

Man's Boasting

Prov. 25:14
Jude 1:12

God's Wrath

Isa. 30:27

Babylonian Army

Jer. 4:13

Club/Rod

False Testimony

Prov. 25:18

God's Wrath

Isa. 10:5

Babylon

Jer. 51:20

Assyria

Isa. 10:5

Coals

Survivor/Heir

2 Sam. 14:7

Cleansing/Holiness

Isa. 6:6
Ezek. 1:13

Divine Anger

2 Sam. 22:9
Ps. 11:6
Ps. 18:8
Ps. 140:10
Ezek. 10:2
Ezek. 24:11

Adultery

Prov. 6:28

Shame/Contrition

Prov. 25:22
Rom. 12:20

Cobwebs

Futility/Failure

Job 8:14–15
Isa. 59:5–6

Cooking

Divine Judgment

Ezek. 11:3
Ezek. 24:1–6
Ezek. 24:10

Cords

(see also Bind/Bound)

Death

2 Sam. 22:6
Job 4:21
Ps. 18:4–5
Ps. 116:3
Eccles. 12:6

Affliction

Job 36:8

Freedom

Ps. 129:4

Sin

Prov. 5:22
Isa. 5:18

Expansion

Isa. 54:2

True Fasting

Isa. 58:6

God's Kindness

Hosea 11:4

Cornerstone

Leaders

Isa. 19:13

Messiah

Isa. 28:16
Zech. 10:4
Eph. 2:20
1 Peter 2:6

Court/Trial

Meeting God in Court

Job 9:3
Job 9:14–16
Job 9:19–20
Job 9:28–35
Job 10:2
Job 13:6–8
Job 13:19
Job 16:19–21
Prov. 22:22–23
Isa. 3:13
Dan. 7:10
Dan. 7:26

Human Judgment

1 Cor. 4:3

Cows/Heifer

Selfish Women

Amos 4:1–3

A Bride

Judg. 14:18

Egypt

Jer. 46:20

Cream
(see also Milk)

Prosperity
Job 29:6

Creation

Like Birth
Job 15:7
Job 38:8–9
Job 38:28–29
Ps. 90:2

Like a Building or Tent
1 Sam. 2:8
2 Sam. 22:8
2 Sam. 22:16
Job 38:4–6
Ps. 18:7
Ps. 18:15
Ps. 19:4
Ps. 24:2
Ps. 82:5
Ps. 102:25
Ps. 104:2
Ps. 104:5
Prov. 3:19
Prov. 8:29
Isa. 24:18
Isa. 40:21
Isa. 45:18
Isa. 48:13
Isa. 51:13
Isa. 51:16
Jer. 31:37
Amos 9:6
Micah 6:2
Zech. 12:1
Heb. 1:10

Like Salvation—New Creation in Christ
2 Cor. 5:17
Gal. 6:15
Eph. 2:10
Eph. 4:24

Cross

Obedient Submission
Matt. 10:38
Matt. 16:24
Mark 8:34
Luke 9:23
Luke 14:27
Gal. 5:11
Gal. 6:12

The Atonement
1 Cor. 1:17
Gal. 6:14
Eph. 2:16
Phil. 3:18
Col. 2:15

The Gospel Message
1 Cor. 1:18

Crowns

Honor/Dishonor (Lose Crown)
Job 19:9
Job 31:35–36
Ps. 8:5
Ps. 89:39
Prov. 4:9
Jer. 13:18
Lam. 5:16
Heb. 2:7–9
Rev. 3:11

Material Blessing
Ps. 65:11
Prov. 10:6
Prov. 11:26
Prov. 14:24

A Noble Wife
Prov. 12:4

Gray Hair
Prov. 16:31

Grandchildren
Prov. 17:6

The Lord
Isa. 28:5

Salvation
Ps. 149:4

Joy
Isa. 35:10
Isa. 51:11

Beauty
Isa. 61:3

Israel
Isa. 62:3

Rewards
1 Cor. 9:25
2 Tim. 2:5
2 Tim. 4:8
James 1:12
1 Peter 5:4
Rev. 2:10
Rev. 4:4
Rev. 4:10

God's People
Phil. 4:1
1 Thess. 2:19

Knowledge
Prov. 14:18

Love/Mercy

Ps. 103:4

Crucible

(see Furnace)

Cups

God's Will/Inheritance

Ps. 16:5
Matt. 20:22–23
Matt. 26:39
Matt. 26:42
Mark 10:38–39
Mark 14:36
Luke 22:42
John 18:11

Abundant Blessing

Ps. 23:5

Judgment

Job 21:20
Ps. 75:8
Isa. 51:17
Isa. 51:22
Jer. 25:15
Jer. 25:17
Jer. 25:28
Jer. 49:12
Jer. 51:7
Lam. 4:21
Ezek. 23:31–33
Hab. 2:16
Rev. 14:10
Rev. 16:19
Rev. 18:6

Christ's Blood

Matt. 26:27
Luke 22:20
1 Cor. 10:16
1 Cor. 10:21
1 Cor. 11:25

Salvation

Ps. 116:13

Bablyon

Jer. 51:7

Jerusalem

Zech. 12:2

Hypocrisy

Matt. 23:25–26
Luke 11:39

Martyrdom/ Persecution

Rev. 17:4

D

Darkness

Sin

Ps. 82:5
Prov. 2:13
Prov. 4:19–20
Isa. 5:20
Isa. 29:15
Ezek. 8:12
Matt. 6:23
Luke 11:34
John 3:19–21
John 8:12
Acts 26:18

Discouragement/ Trouble

Job 23:17
Job 30:26
Ps. 88:12
Ps. 88:18
Ps. 107:10
Ps. 107:14
Isa. 9:2
Isa. 42:16
Isa. 50:10
Isa. 59:9
Lam. 3:2
Lam. 3:6
Matt. 4:16
Luke 1:79

Judgment

Exod. 10:21
Deut. 4:11
Deut. 5:22–23
Josh. 24:7
1 Sam. 2:9
Job 5:14
Job 15:22–23
Job 15:30
Ps. 18:9
Ps. 18:11
Ps. 69:23
Ps. 105:28
Ezek. 32:7–8
Joel 2:10
Joel 3:15
Amos 5:20
Micah 3:6
Matt. 24:29
Mark 13:24
Rom. 11:10
2 Peter 2:17
Jude 1:6
Jude 1:13
Rev. 9:2
Rev. 16:10

Ignorance

Isa. 8:20
John 1:5
Rom. 1:21
Eph. 4:18

Satan/Satan's Kingdom

Luke 22:53
John 13:27–30
Eph. 6:12
Col. 1:13

Death

Job 3:4–6
Job 3:9
Job 18:6
Job 18:18
Prov. 20:20
Eccles. 6:4

Old Age

Eccles. 12:2

Evil World System

2 Peter 1:19

God's Covering

2 Sam 22:12
Ps. 18:11
Ps. 97:2

Dawn

(see Sun/Dawning)

Debt

(see also Account/Impute)

Sin

Lev. 26:41
Lev. 26:43
Isa. 40:2
Matt. 6:12
Luke 7:40–43

Love

Rom. 13:8

Appreciation

Ps. 116:12
Rom. 11:35
Philem. 1:19

Retribution

Gen. 50:15
Deut. 7:10
Deut. 32:35
Deut. 32:41
2 Sam. 3:39
1 Kings 2:32
1 Kings 2:44
2 Chron. 6:23
2 Chron. 20:11
Ps. 28:4
Ps. 31:23
Ps. 35:12
Ps. 38:20
Ps. 41:10
Ps. 69:22
Ps. 94:23
Ps. 109:5
Ps. 109:20
Ps. 137:8
Prov. 17:13
Prov. 24:12
Isa. 35:4
Isa. 59:18
Isa. 65:6–7
Isa. 66:6
Jer. 16:18
Jer. 25:14
Jer. 50:29
Jer. 51:6
Jer. 51:24
Jer. 51:56
Lam. 3:64
Ezek. 7:3
Ezek. 7:8–9
Hosea 4:9
Hosea 12:2
Hosea 12:14
Joel 3:4
Rom. 12:17
1 Thess. 5:15
2 Thess. 1:6
2 Tim. 4:14
Rev. 18:6

Reward

Ruth 2:12
2 Sam. 16:12
Joel 2:25
Rev. 2:23

Grace

Ps. 103:10
Joel 2:25
1 Peter 3:9

Discipline

Isa. 50:1

Decay

Disgraceful Wife

Prov. 12:4

Envy

Prov. 14:30

Awe

Hab. 3:13

Deer

Desire for God

Ps. 42:1

Power from God

2 Sam. 22:34
Ps. 18:33
Hab. 3:19

A Faithful Wife

Prov. 5:19

Yielding to Temptation

Prov. 7:22

Weakness, Defeat

Isa. 51:20
Lam. 1:6

The Beloved

Song of Sol. 2:9
Song of Sol. 2:17

Breasts

Song of Sol. 4:5

Deposit

Holy Spirit

2 Cor. 5:5

Depths

(see also Drown/Sink)

Consequences of Sin

Ps. 130:1
Prov. 9:18
Lam. 3:55
Jonah 2:2

Judgment

Exod. 15:5
Neh. 9:11
Ps. 88:6
Isa. 14:15
Matt. 11:23

God's Mysteries

Job 11:8
Rom. 11:33

Victory/Salvation

Ps. 30:1
Ps. 71:20
Ps. 86:13
Ps. 106:9

Danger/Death

Ps. 69:2
Ps. 69:15

Forgiveness

Micah 7:19

Love

2 Cor. 2:4

Desert

Absence of Blessing

Jer. 2:31

God's Chastening/Judgment

Ps. 107:33
Isa. 50:2
Isa. 64:10
Jer. 4:11
Jer. 22:6
Jer. 50:12
Hosea 2:3
Hosea 13:15
Zeph. 2:14

God's Blessing

Ps. 107:35
Isa. 32:15
Isa. 35:1
Isa. 35:6
Isa. 41:18–19
Isa. 43:19–20
Isa. 51:3

Invaders

Isa. 25:5

Forsaken City

Isa. 27:10

Idolaters

Jer. 3:2

Forsaken/Isolated

Jer. 48:6

Devour

(see Eating/Devouring/Swallowing)

Dew

Blessing/Prosperity

Gen. 27:28
Gen. 27:39
Deut. 33:13
Deut. 33:28
Job 29:19
Hosea 14:5
Zech. 8:12

Resurrection

Isa. 26:19

God's Word

Deut. 32:2

God's People

Micah 5:7

Favor

Prov. 19:12

God's Patience

Isa. 18:4

Insincere Love

Hosea 6:4

Unity

Ps. 133:3

Military Attack

2 Sam. 17:12

Idolaters

Hosea 13:3

Dirt

(see also Dust/Mud, Mud/Mire)

Prosperity

Zech. 9:3

Ruined Reputation/Slander

Job 13:4
Ps. 119:69

Disease/Sickness

Sin

2 Chron. 7:14
Isa. 1:5–6
Isa. 30:26
Isa. 33:24
Isa. 53:5
Jer. 3:22
Jer. 17:14
Jer. 30:17
Jer. 33:6
Hosea 6:1
Hosea 14:4
Luke 5:31

Discouragement

Prov. 13:12

Divorce

God's Discipline of Israel

Isa. 50:1
Jer. 3:8

Dog/Dog's Head

A Nobody, Despised Person

1 Sam. 17:43
1 Sam. 24:14
2 Sam. 3:8
2 Sam. 9:8
2 Sam. 16:9
2 Kings 8:13

Apostates/Fools

Prov. 26:11
2 Peter 2:22

Enemies

Ps. 22:16
Ps. 22:20
Ps. 59:6
Ps. 59:14

Unfaithful Leaders

Isa. 56:10–11

Sinners

Matt. 7:6
Rev. 22:15

Legalists

Phil. 3:2

Gentiles

Matt. 15:26–27
Mark 7:27–28

A Meddler

Prov. 26:17

Ineffective Sacrifices

Isa. 66:3

Donkey

Ishmael

Gen. 16:12

The Poor

Job 24:5

Sinners (Seeking Idols)

Jer. 2:24

Israel (Seeking Help)

Hosea 8:9

Stubbornness

Ps. 32:9
Prov. 26:3

Tribe of Issachar

Gen. 49:14

Disgrace

Jer. 22:19

Instinct/Recognition

Isa. 1:3

Door/Gate

Temptation

Gen. 4:7

Generosity

Job 31:32

Speech

Ps. 141:3

Laziness

Prov. 26:14

Preparation for Marriage

Song of Sol. 8:9

Hope

Hosea 2:15

Solitude

Matt. 6:6

Prayer

Matt. 7:7–8
Luke 11:9

Return of Christ

Matt. 24:33
Mark 13:29
James 5:9

Determination

Luke 13:24–25

Opportunity

1 Cor. 16:9
2 Cor. 2:12
Col. 4:3
Rev. 3:8
Rev. 3:20

Christ

John 10:1–9

Death (Door Shut)

Job 3:10

Rejection

Heb. 13:12

Deafness

Eccles. 12:4

God's Providence

Job 38:8
Job 38:10
Isa. 45:1

False Teaching

Matt. 23:13

Dove

Gen. 8:8

A Loved One

Ps. 74:19
Song of Sol. 2:14
Song of Sol. 5:2
Song of Sol. 6:9

The Holy Spirit

Gen. 1:2
Matt. 3:16

Mark 1:10
Luke 3:22
John 1:32–33

Security

Jer. 48:28

Sorrow

Isa. 38:14
Ezek. 7:16
Nahum 2:7

Innocence

Hosea 7:11
Matt. 10:16

Fright

Hosea 11:11

Gentleness/Beauty

Song of Sol. 1:15
Song of Sol. 4:1
Song of Sol. 5:12

Homing Instinct

Isa. 60:8

Dragon

(see Serpent/Dragon)

Dream/Dreamers

Brevity of Life

Job 20:8

Vain Lives of Sinners

Ps. 73:20

False Confidence

Isa. 29:7–8

Unexpected Favor

Ps. 126:1

False Teachers

Jude 1:8

Drift

(see Ship/Shipwreck/Drift)

Drinking

(see also Water/Well [for drinking])

Illicit Love

Prov. 7:18
Prov. 9:17

Married Love

Prov. 5:15–18
Song of Sol. 5:1

Receiving Salvation

Prov. 9:5
Isa. 12:3
Isa. 66:11
John 4:10–14
John 6:53
John 6:55
John 7:37
Rev. 21:6

Doing God's Will

Matt. 20:22–23
Mark 10:38–39
John 18:11

Sin/Disobedience

Job 15:16
Job 34:7
Prov. 4:17
Rev. 14:8

Prosperity

Isa. 60:16

Unbelief

Jer. 2:18

Punishment

Jer. 8:14
Jer. 9:15
Jer. 23:15
Jer. 25:15–17
Ezek. 23:32–34
Obad. 1:16
Rev. 14:10

Inner Pain

Job 6:4

Dross

(see also Furnace)

Wicked People

Ps. 119:119

Spiritual Decay

Isa. 1:22
Isa. 1:25
Jer. 6:27–30
Ezek. 22:18–19

Tests in Life

Prov. 17:3
Prov. 27:21

Drown/Sink

Affliction

2 Sam. 22:5–7
Job 10:15
Ps. 18:4–6
Ps. 69:2
Ps. 69:14

Punishment

Deut. 28:43
Jer. 51:64
Ezek. 27:27

Amos 8:8
Amos 9:5

Guilt

Ezra 9:6
Ps. 130:1–4

Drunk/Drunkenness

(see also Wine/Wine Press)

Divine Judgment

Job 12:25
Isa. 19:14
Isa. 24:20
Isa. 49:26
Isa. 51:17
Isa. 51:21
Isa. 52:22
Isa. 63:6
Jer. 13:13
Jer. 25:27
Jer. 48:26
Jer. 51:7
Jer. 51:39
Jer. 51:57
Lam. 4:21
Ezek. 23:33
Ezek. 39:19
Nahum 1:10
Nahum 3:11

Spiritual Excitement

Acts 2:13–15
Eph. 5:18

Retribution

Rev. 16:5–6

Martyrdom

Rev. 17:6

Worldly Influence to Sin

Rev. 14:8
Rev. 17:2
Rev. 17:4
Rev. 18:3
Rev. 18:9

Dung/Manure/Refuse

(see also Offal)

Divine Judgment

1 Kings 14:10
2 Kings 9:37
Job 20:7
Ps. 83:10
Isa. 5:25
Isa. 25:10
Jer. 8:1–2
Jer. 9:22
Jer. 16:14
Jer. 25:33
Lam. 3:45
Zeph. 1:17

Dust/Mud

Humiliation

Gen. 3:14
Gen. 3:19
Gen. 18:27
1 Sam. 2:8
2 Sam. 22:43
2 Kings 13:7
Job 16:15
Job 30:19
Job 42:6
Ps. 18:42
Ps. 44:25
Ps. 72:9
Ps. 89:39
Ps. 103:14
Ps. 119:25
Isa. 47:1
Isa. 49:23
Jer. 17:13
Lam. 3:16
Lam. 3:29
Micah 7:17

Multiplication

Gen. 13:16
Gen. 28:14
Num. 23:10
2 Chron. 1:9
Ps. 78:27

Death

Gen. 3:19
Job 7:21
Job 10:9
Job 17:16
Job 20:11
Job 21:26
Job 34:15
Ps. 7:5
Ps. 22:15
Ps. 90:3
Ps. 104:29
Eccles. 3:20
Eccles. 12:7
Isa. 26:19
Dan. 12:2
Zeph. 1:17

Wealth

Job 27:16
Zech. 9:3

Poverty

Ps. 22:29

Judgment—Defeat

Isa. 5:24
Isa. 25:12
Isa. 26:5
Isa. 29:5
Matt. 10:14
Mark 6:11
Luke 9:5
Luke 10:11
Acts 13:51

Insignificance

Isa. 40:15
Isa. 41:2

Promotion

1 Kings 16:1

E

Eagle

Swiftness

Deut. 28:49
2 Sam. 1:23
Jer. 4:13
Lam. 4:19
Obad. 1:4

Vanishing Wealth

Prov. 23:5

Security/Heights

Job 39:27–28
Jer. 49:16

God's Leading

Exod. 19:4
Deut. 32:11

Invasion

Job 9:26
Jer. 48:40
Jer. 49:22
Ezek. 17:3
Ezek. 17:7
Hosea 8:1

Angelic Creatures

Ezek. 1:10
Ezek. 10:14
Dan. 7:6
Rev. 4:7

Deliverance

Rev. 12:14

Renewal

Isa. 40:31

Swiftness of Life

Job 9:26

Earring

Wise Rebuke

Prov. 25:12

Ears/Hearing

Desire for Novelty (Itching Ears)

2 Tim. 4:3

Hear Shocking News (Ears Tingle)

1 Sam. 3:11
2 Kings 21:12
Jer. 19:3

Submission

Exod. 21:6
Deut. 15:17
Ps. 40:6

Spiritual Inattention

Zech. 7:11
2 Tim. 4:4

Spiritual Deafness

Deut. 29:4
Ps. 58:4
Isa. 6:10
Isa. 42:20
Isa. 43:8
Jer. 5:21
Jer. 6:10
Ezek. 12:2
Matt. 13:15–16
Mark 8:18
Acts 7:51
Acts 28:27
Rom. 11:8

Unconcern

Prov. 21:13
Isa. 33:15
Lam. 3:56
Acts 7:57

Earthquake/ Quake

National Upheaval

Ps. 60:2

God's Help/Presence

Ps. 18:7
Ps. 77:18

Fear

1 Sam. 13:7

Eating/ Devouring/ Swallowing

Death (Sword Devours)

Deut. 32:42
2 Sam. 1:22

2 Sam. 2:26
2 Sam. 11:25
Isa. 1:20
Isa. 31:8
Jer. 2:30
Jer. 5:17
Jer. 8:16
Jer. 12:12
Jer. 46:10
Jer. 46:14
Nahum 2:13

Defeat/Conquest (Land Devours)

Exod. 15:12
Lev. 26:38
Num. 14:9
Num. 16:30–32
Num. 23:24
Num. 24:8
Num. 26:10
Deut. 11:6
2 Sam. 17:16
2 Sam. 20:19–20
Ps. 106:17
Isa. 9:12
Isa. 49:19
Jer. 2:3
Jer. 10:25
Jer. 30:16
Jer. 51:34
Jer. 51:44
Lam. 2:16
Ezek. 19:3
Ezek. 19:6
Ezek. 35:12
Ezek. 36:13–14
Dan. 7:7
Dan. 7:19
Dan. 7:23
Hosea 8:8
Hab. 1:13

Divine Wrath

Deut. 32:22
Job 37:20
Ps. 21:9
Ps. 44:11
Ps. 50:3
Ps. 79:7
Isa. 34:5–6
Jer. 12:12
Lam. 2:2
Lam. 2:5
Ezek. 7:15
Hosea 13:8
Amos 5:6

Human Oppression (Greed)

Job 20:15
Ps. 14:4
Ps. 27:2
Ps. 35:25
Ps. 53:4
Prov. 30:14
Ezek. 22:25
Micah 3:1–3
Mark 12:40
Luke 20:47
Gal. 5:15

Assassination

Hosea 7:7

Satanic Attack

1 Peter 5:8
Rev. 12:4

Poverty

Prov. 21:20

Crime/Murder

Prov. 1:12

Victory Over Death

Isa. 25:8
1 Cor. 15:54
2 Cor. 5:4

Hypocrisy

Matt. 23:24

Compromise

Hosea 8:8

Folly

Prov. 15:14

Joyful Heart

Prov. 15:15

Commit Sin

Prov. 19:28

The Grave

Isa. 5:14

Exploitation

Hosea 3:8

Ebbing (Away)

Slow Death

Job 30:16
Ps. 107:3
Lam. 2:12
Jonah 2:7

Eden

Restoration, Renewal

Isa. 51:3
Ezek. 36:35

Devastation

Joel 2:3

Eggs

Nations

Isa. 10:13–14

Lies

Isa. 59:5

Egypt

False Security (The "World")

Gen. 12:10
Gen. 26:2
Num. 11:5
Num. 11:18
Num. 11:20
Num. 14:2–4
Num. 20:5
Num. 21:5
Deut. 17:16
Isa. 31:1–3
Jer. 42:13–19
Jer. 43:2

Like Flies (The Enemy)

Isa. 7:18

Like a Furnace

Deut. 4:20

Like a Garment

Jer. 43:12

Like a Heifer

Jer. 46:20

Jerusalem

Rev. 11:8

Like a River

Jer. 46:8

Like a Serpent

Jer. 46:22

Engraving

Sin

Jer. 17:1

Divine Remembrance

Isa. 49:16

Exodus

Death

Luke 9:31
2 Peter 1:15

Eye/Eyes

Special Affection/ Treasure

Deut. 32:10
Ps. 17:8
Prov. 7:2
Zech. 2:8

Evil Plotting

Ps. 35:19
Prov. 6:13
Prov. 16:30

Singleness of Purpose

Prov. 4:25
Matt. 6:22–23
Luke 11:34

Acceptance

Gen. 6:8
Gen. 18:3
Gen. 19:19
Gen. 30:27
Gen. 32:5
Gen. 33:8
Gen. 33:10
Gen. 33:15
Gen. 34:11
Gen. 39:4
Gen. 47:25
Gen. 47:29
Gen. 50:4
Exod. 34:9
Num. 11:15
Num. 32:5
Judg. 6:17
Ruth 2:2
Ruth 2:10
Ruth 2:13
1 Sam. 1:18
1 Sam. 20:3
1 Sam. 20:29
1 Sam. 27:5
1 Sam. 29:9
2 Sam. 14:22
2 Sam. 15:25
2 Sam. 16:4

Rejection

Exod. 8:26
Deut. 24:4

Bribery

Deut. 16:19
1 Sam. 12:3

Disappointment

Deut. 28:32
Deut. 28:65
Ps. 69:3
Ps. 88:9
Ps. 119:82
Ps. 123:1–4
Lam. 4:17

Strength/ Encouragement

1 Sam. 14:27
1 Sam. 14:29
Ps. 13:3

Humility

1 Sam. 15:17

Pride

2 Kings 19:22
Ps. 18:27
Ps. 101:5
Ps. 131:1

Prov. 3:7
Prov. 6:17
Prov. 21:4
Prov. 26:5
Prov. 26:12
Prov. 26:16
Prov. 28:11
Prov. 30:13
Isa. 2:11
Isa. 5:15
Isa. 5:21
Isa. 10:12
Isa. 37:23
Micah 4:11
Rom. 3:18

Wisdom

Ps. 19:8
Ps. 119:18
Ezek. 10:12
Zech. 3:9
Zech. 4:10
Rev. 4:6
Rev. 4:8

Weakness

Ps. 38:10
Lam. 5:17

Expectations

2 Chron. 20:12
Ps. 121:1
Ps. 123:1–2
Ps. 141:8
Ps. 145:15

Discernment

Prov. 20:8
Eph. 1:18

Discontent

Eccles. 4:8

Appetite

Eccles. 5:11
Ezek. 20:24
2 Peter 2:14
1 John 2:16

Wife

Ezek. 24:16
Ezek. 24:21

Faith

Heb. 12:2

God's Holy Judgment

Rev. 1:14
Rev. 2:18
Rev. 19:12

F

Face

Banishment (Not See the Face)

Gen. 43:3
Gen. 43:5
Gen. 44:23
Gen. 44:26
Exod. 10:28
Deut. 31:17–18
2 Sam. 14:24
2 Sam. 14:28
2 Chron. 30:9
Job 13:24
Job 32:29
Ps. 13:1
Ps. 22:24
Ps. 27:9
Ps. 30:7
Ps. 34:16
Ps. 44:24
Ps. 69:17
Ps. 88:14
Ps. 102:2
Ps. 104:29
Ps. 143:7
Isa. 8:17
Isa. 54:8
Isa. 57:17
Isa. 59:2
Isa. 64:7
Jer. 18:17
Jer. 33:5
Ezek. 7:22
Ezek. 39:23
Ezek. 39:29
Micah 3:4
1 Peter 3:12

Reverence (Hide the Face)

Exod. 3:6
1 Kings 19:13

Resistance (Set the Face Against)

Lev. 17:10
Lev. 20:3
Lev. 20:5
Lev. 26:17
Ezek. 6:2
Ezek. 13:17
Ezek. 14:8
Ezek. 15:7
Ezek. 21:2
Ezek. 25:2
Ezek. 28:21
Ezek. 29:2
Ezek. 38:2

Acceptance/Blessing (Face Shine on You)

Num. 6:25
Ps. 4:6
Ps. 31:16
Ps. 44:3
Ps. 67:1
Ps. 80:3
Ps. 80:7
Ps. 80:19
Ps. 119:135
Prov. 16:15

Shame (Slap/Spit in the Face)

Num. 12:14
Deut. 25:9
1 Kings 22:24
2 Chron. 18:23
Job 17:6
Job 30:10
Ps. 44:15
Ps. 69:7
Nahum 3:5
2 Cor. 11:20

Grief (Face to the Wall, Cover the Face)

2 Sam. 19:4
2 Kings 20:2
Isa. 38:2

Devotion (Seek God's Face)

2 Sam. 21:1
1 Chron. 16:11
2 Chron. 7:14
Ps. 24:6
Ps. 27:8
Ps. 105:4
Ps. 119:58
Hosea 5:15

Condemnation

Esther 7:8
Rev. 6:16

Prosperity

Job 15:27

Forgiveness

Ps. 51:9

Determination

Isa. 50:7

Courage

1 Chron. 12:8

Father

Tender Care

Deut. 1:31
Job 29:16
Ps. 103:13
1 Thess. 2:11
1 Tim. 5:1

God (to Israel)

Deut. 32:6
Deut. 32:18
2 Sam. 7:14
1 Chron. 17:13
1 Chron. 22:10
1 Chron. 28:6
Isa. 9:6
Isa. 63:16
Isa. 64:8
Jer. 3:4
Jer. 3:19
Jer. 31:9
Mal. 1:6
Mal. 2:10

Spiritual Leaders

Judg. 17:10
Judg. 18:19
2 Kings 2:12
2 Kings 6:21
2 Kings 13:14
Phil. 2:22

Other Leaders

2 Kings 5:13
Isa. 22:21

The Grave

Job 17:14

Idols

Jer. 2:27

Satan

John 8:44

Abraham

Rom. 4:12
Rom. 4:16–18

Feast

Messianic Kingdom

Ps. 22:29
Isa. 25:6
Matt. 8:11
Luke 13:29
Luke 14:15

Spiritual Delights

Ps. 36:8

Cheerfulness/Joy

Prov. 15:15
Lam. 2:7

Judgment

Jer. 51:39
Lam. 2:22
Ezek. 39:17–20
Rev. 19:17–21

Feet/Foot

Conquest (Under Feet)

Josh. 10:24
1 Kings 5:3
2 Kings 19:24
Ps. 8:6
Ps. 45:5
Ps. 47:3
Ps. 58:10
Ps. 68:23
Ps. 110:1
Isa. 37:25
Mal. 4:3
Matt. 22:44
Mark 12:36
Luke 20:43
Acts 2:35
Rom. 16:20
1 Cor. 15:25
1 Cor. 15:27
Eph. 1:22
Heb. 1:13
Heb. 2:8

Prosperity

Deut. 33:24

Marriage Proposal

Ruth 3:4
Ruth 3:7

Protection

1 Sam. 2:9
Ps. 36:11
Ps. 91:12
Ps. 94:18
Ps. 121:3
Prov. 3:23
Prov. 3:26
Matt. 4:6
Luke 4:11

Enablement

2 Sam. 22:34
Ps. 18:33
Ps. 44:18
Hab. 3:19

Judgment/Trial

Job 13:27
Job 18:8
Job 30:12

Job 33:11
Ps. 9:5
Ps. 25:15
Ps. 57:6
Ps. 140:4
Prov. 29:5
Jer. 18:22
Lam. 1:13

Good News

Isa. 52:7
Nahum 1:15
Rom. 10:15

Rejection

Matt. 10:14
Mark 6:11
Luke 9:5
Luke 10:11
Acts 13:51

Spiritual Cleansing/ Humility

John 13:8–10
John 13:13–16

Faith

Gen. 13:17
Deut. 11:24
Josh. 1:3

Unfaithful People

Prov. 25:19

Apostasy

Heb. 10:29

Figs/Fig Tree

Vulnerability

Isa. 28:4
Nahum 3:12

Delight

Hosea 9:10

Compensation

Prov. 27:18

Security

1 Kings 4:25
2 Kings 18:31
Isa. 36:16
Micah 4:4
Zech. 3:10

Judgment

Isa. 34:4
Rev. 6:13

Jewish Exiles

Jer. 24:1–7

Survivors in Jerusalem

Jer. 24:8–10

Finger

Divine Power

Exod. 8:19
Ps. 8:3
Luke 11:20

Revelation of Word

Exod. 31:18
Exod. 32:16
Deut. 9:10
Dan. 5:5

Boasting

1 Kings 12:10
2 Chron. 10:10

Obedience

Prov. 7:3

Fire/Burning

Divine Anger

Exod. 4:14
Exod. 15:7
Exod. 32:10–12
Num. 11:33
Num. 12:9
Num. 25:3–4
Num. 32:13
Deut. 6:15
Deut. 7:4
Deut. 11:17
Deut. 29:24
Deut. 29:27
Josh. 7:1
Josh. 23:16
Judg. 3:8
2 Sam. 6:7
2 Sam. 24:1
2 Kings 13:3
2 Kings 22:13
2 Kings 22:17
2 Kings 23:26
1 Chron. 13:10
2 Chron. 25:15
Job 4:9
Job 19:11
Job 20:23
Ps. 74:1
Ps. 78:49
Ps. 80:4
Isa. 5:25
Isa. 13:13
Isa. 30:27
Isa. 30:30
Isa. 42:25
Jer. 15:14
Jer. 17:4
Ezek. 22:31
Ezek. 38:18
Hosea 8:5
Amos 5:6
Zeph. 3:8
Zech. 10:3

Human Anger

Gen. 39:19
Exod. 11:8
Exod. 32:19
Num. 24:10
Judg. 14:19
1 Sam. 11:6
1 Sam. 17:28
1 Sam. 20:30
2 Sam. 6:7
2 Sam. 11:20
Esther 1:12
Ps. 124:3

Hell

Matt. 5:22
Matt. 13:40–42
Matt. 18:9
Matt. 25:41
Mark 9:43
Mark 9:45
Mark 9:47–49

Persecution

Luke 12:49

God's Providential Presence

Exod. 3:2
Exod. 19:18
Deut. 9:3

Firstfruits

The Best People

Ps. 78:51
Ps. 105:36

Israel

Jer. 2:3

Holy Spirit

Rom. 8:23

The Resurrected Christ

1 Cor. 15:20
1 Cor. 15:23

God's People

James 1:18
Rev. 14:4

Fish/Fishermen

Unpredictability of Life

Eccles. 9:12

War Victims

Amos 4:1–2
Hab. 1:14–15

Conquering Armies

Jer. 16:16

Evangelists

Matt. 4:19
Mark 1:17

Flies

Egypt

Isa. 7:18

Death

Isa. 51:6

Flint

Determination

Isa. 50:7
Ezek. 3:9

Inattention/Rebellion

Jer. 5:3
Zech. 7:11–12

Flock

(see Lamb, Sheep/Flock)

Flood (Noah)

Baptism

1 Peter 3:20–21

Unpreparedness

Matt. 24:36–39

Floodgates

Judgment from Heaven

Gen. 7:11
Gen. 8:2
Isa. 24:18
Luke 4:25

Blessing from Heaven

2 Kings 7:2
2 Kings 7:19
Ps. 78:23–24
Mal. 3:10

Floods

(see also Drown/Sink, Water [as a Flood])

Terrors

Job 27:20
Ps. 88:16–17

Tears

Ps. 6:6
Mal. 2:13

Attack

Ps. 69:15
Ps. 124:1–5
Dan. 9:26

Dan. 11:10
Dan. 11:40

Divine Wrath

Ps. 42:7
Isa. 8:7
Isa. 28:2
Isa. 59:19
Hosea 5:10
Nahum 1:8

Excessive Sin

1 Peter 4:4

Trouble

Ps. 32:6

Wealth

Isa. 66:12

Satanic Attack

Rev. 12:16

Flower

(see also Grass, Plant)

Brevity of Life

Job 14:2
Ps. 103:15

Fading Glory

Isa. 28:1
Isa. 28:4
Isa. 40:6–8
James 1:10
1 Peter 1:24

Judgment

Isa. 5:24

Flute

A Grieving Heart

Jer. 48:36

Food

(see also Eating/Devouring/Swallowing)

Evil

Job 20:12–15
Prov. 4:17

God's Word

Deut. 8:3
Job 23:12
Ps. 119:103
Ezek. 2:8
Ezek. 3:1–3
Amos 8:11
Matt. 4:4
Luke 4:4
1 Cor. 3:1–2
Heb. 5:12–14
1 Peter 2:2
Rev. 10:9–10

Destroying the Innocent

Ps. 14:4
Ps. 53:4

Sorrow

Ps. 42:3
Ps. 80:5
Ps. 102:9
Isa. 30:20

Faith

Eccles. 11:1

Christ's Body/Flesh

Matt. 26:26
Mark 14:22
John 6:33
John 6:35
John 6:41
John 6:48
John 6:51
John 6:58
1 Cor. 11:23–24

Sincerity

1 Cor. 5:8

Judgment

Jer. 9:15
Jer. 23:15
Dan. 4:25
Dan. 4:32

God's Will

John 4:32
John 4:34

Consequences

Ps. 128:2
Prov. 1:31
Prov. 13:25
Prov. 18:21

Stolen Pleasure

Prov. 9:17
Prov. 20:17

Footstool

The Ark/Temple of God

1 Chron. 28:2
Ps. 99:5
Ps. 132:7
Lam. 2:1

Planet Earth

Isa. 66:1
Matt. 5:35
Acts 7:49

Conquest

Ps. 110:1
Luke 20:43
Acts 2:35

Eph. 1:22
Heb. 1:13
Heb. 2:6–9
Heb. 10:13

Fortress

(see also Rock/Stone, Tower/Fortress)

Security in God

2 Sam. 22:2
Ps. 18:2
Ps. 28:8
Ps. 31:2–3
Ps. 46:7
Ps. 46:11
Ps. 48:3
Ps. 59:9
Ps. 59:16–17
Ps. 62:2
Ps. 62:6
Ps. 71:3
Ps. 91:2
Ps. 94:22
Ps. 144:2
Prov. 14:26
Isa. 17:10
Jer. 16:19
Zech. 9:12

Foundation

(see also Building/ Builders, Rock/Stone)

Creation

1 Sam. 2:8
2 Sam. 22:8
2 Sam. 22:16
Job 38:4
Ps. 18:15
Ps. 24:2
Ps. 82:5
Ps. 89:11
Ps. 102:25
Ps. 104:5
Prov. 3:19
Prov. 8:29
Isa. 24:18
Isa. 40:21
Isa. 45:18
Isa. 48:13
Isa. 51:13
Isa. 51:16
Jer. 10:12
Jer. 31:37
Jer. 51:15
Micah 6:2
Zech. 12:1
Heb. 1:10

Justice

Ps. 89:14
Ps. 97:2

The Temple

Ps. 87:1

Christ

Isa. 28:16

God

Isa. 33:6

Obedience to God

Matt. 7:25
Luke 6:48–49

Ministry

Rom. 15:20
1 Cor. 3:10–12
Eph. 2:20

The Church

1 Tim. 3:15
2 Tim. 2:19

Stewardship

1 Tim. 6:19

Basic Doctrine

Heb. 6:1

God's Wrath

Deut. 32:22
2 Sam. 22:8
2 Sam. 22:16
Job 22:16
Ps. 18:7
Ps. 18:15
Isa. 24:18

Social Decay

Ps. 11:3
Ps. 82:5

God's Promises

Heb. 8:6

Fountain

Life from God

Ps. 36:9
Ps. 87:7
Jer. 2:13
Jer. 17:13

A Godly Wife

Prov. 5:18

Righteous Words

Prov. 10:11

Wisdom

Prov. 13:14
Prov. 16:22
Prov. 18:4

Fear of the Lord

Prov. 14:27

Cleansing from Sin

Zech. 13:1

Fragrance/ Incense
(see also Stench)

Pleasing God

Gen. 8:21
Exod. 29:18
Exod. 29:25
Lev. 1:9
Lev. 1:13
Lev. 2:9
Lev. 4:31
Num. 15:3
Num. 15:7

Christ's Sacrifice

Eph. 5:2

Christian Witness

2 Cor. 2:14–16

Gifts Presented to God

John 12:3–8
Phil. 4:18

Prayer

Ps. 141:2
Rev. 5:8
Rev. 8:4

Restoration

Hosea 14:5–6

God's Acceptance

Ezek. 20:41

A Good Name

Eccles. 7:1
Song of Sol. 1:3

Complacency

Jer. 48:11

Frogs

Evil Spirit

Rev. 16:13

Fruit

Fulfillment of God's Plan

2 Sam. 23:5

Children

Deut. 7:13
Deut. 28:4
Deut. 28:11
Deut. 28:18
Deut. 28:53
Deut. 30:9
Ps. 128:3
Micah 6:7

Godly Life/Character

Ps. 1:3
Isa. 11:1
Jer. 11:19
Amos 6:12
Matt. 3:8
Matt. 3:10
Matt. 7:16–20
Matt. 12:33
Luke 3:8–9
Luke 6:43–44
John 15:2
John 15:4–5
John 15:8
John 15:16
Rom. 7:4
Gal. 5:22–23
Eph. 5:9
Phil. 1:11
Col. 1:10
James 3:17

Consequences

Prov. 1:31
Isa. 3:10
Jer. 6:19
Ezek. 17:8–9
Ezek. 17:23
Ezek. 19:12
Ezek. 19:14
Hosea 9:16
Hosea 10:13
Rom. 7:5

Words

Prov. 12:14
Prov. 13:2
Prov. 13:20
Hosea 14:2
Heb. 13:15

Delight

Song of Sol. 2:3

Breasts

Song of Sol. 7:7

Peace

Isa. 32:17
Gal. 5:22

Love

Hosea 10:12
Gal. 5:22

Deception

Hosea 10:13

Offerings/Money

Rom. 15:28

Ministry/Converts

Matt. 7:16–20
Luke 6:43–45
Phil. 1:22
Col. 1:6

Fuel

People (Judgment)

Isa. 9:19
Ezek. 21:32

War Material

Isa. 9:5
Ezek. 39:9–10

Furnace

(see also Oven)

Divine Judgment

Gen. 19:28
Exod. 19:18
Ps. 21:9
Isa. 31:9
Ezek. 22:18
Ezek. 22:20
Ezek. 22:22
Mal. 4:1
Rev. 1:15

Affliction

Deut. 4:20
1 Kings 8:51
Isa. 48:10
Jer. 11:4

Testing (Refined)

Ps. 66:10
Prov. 17:3
Prov. 27:21
Isa. 48:10
Jer. 6:27–30
Jer. 9:7
Dan. 11:35
Mal. 3:3

Hell

Matt. 13:42
Matt. 13:50
Rev. 9:2

Purity of the Word

Ps. 12:6

G

Gall

Bitter Consequences of Sin

Prov. 5:4
Eccles. 7:6

Persecution

Ps. 69:21
Lam. 3:15
Lam. 3:19

Anger

1 Sam. 18:8

Garden

A Bride

Song of Sol. 4:12

Judgment

Isa. 1:30
Lam. 2:6
Joel 2:3

Judah/Israel

Num. 24:6
Isa. 5:7

Restoration

Isa. 51:3
Isa. 58:11
Jer. 31:12
Ezek. 36:35

Garland

Wisdom

Prov. 1:9
Prov. 4:9

Garment

(see also Clothing)

Persons Wasting Away

Job 13:28
Isa. 50:9
Isa. 51:8

Creation Decaying

Ps. 102:26
Isa. 51:6
Heb. 1:11–12

God

Job 30:18

Clouds

Job 38:9

Planet Earth

Job 38:14

Light

Ps. 104:2

Seas

Ps. 104:6

Cursing

Ps. 109:18

Lack of Discernment

Prov. 25:20

Praise

Isa. 61:3

God's Victory

Isa. 59:17
Isa. 63:1–3
Jer. 43:12

Violence

Mal. 2:16

Prosperity

Gen. 49:11

God's Splendor

Isa. 52:1

Salvation

Isa. 61:10
Matt. 9:16
Mark 2:21
Luke 5:36

Sin

Isa. 64:6

Gates

Conquest

Gen. 24:60
Ps. 107:16
Isa. 45:2
Amos 1:5
Matt. 16:18

A Meeting Place with God

Gen. 28:17

Demands of Salvation

Matt. 7:13–14

Jesus the Savior

John 10:7
John 10:9

Rejection (Outside the Gate)

Heb. 13:12

Death

Job 17:16
Job 38:17
Ps. 9:13
Ps. 107:18
Isa. 38:10

Disputes

Prov. 18:19

Glaze

Hypocrisy

Prov. 26:23

Gnat

Hypocrisy, Overscrupulousness

Matt. 23:24

Goads

Wise Words

Eccles. 12:11

Resisting God

Acts 26:14

Gold

God's Word

Ps. 19:10
Ps. 119:127

God

Job 22:25

Purifying of Life

Job 23:10
Prov. 17:3
Mal. 3:3
1 Peter 1:7

Wisdom

Prov. 3:14
Prov. 8:10
Prov. 8:19
Prov. 16:16
1 Cor. 3:12

An Indiscreet Woman

Prov. 11:22

A Good Name

Prov. 22:1

Apt Words

Prov. 25:11–12

Praise

Prov. 27:21

Consequences of Sin

Lam. 4:1–2

True Values

Rev. 3:18

Grain/Sheaves

Defeat

Jer. 50:26

Death

Job 5:26
Job 24:24
Jer. 9:22

Discipline

Prov. 27:22

Judgment

Isa. 17:4–5
Jer. 50:26

God's Word

Jer. 23:28

God's Blessing

Hosea 14:7

Grass

Human Frailty

2 Kings 19:26
Job 8:12
Job 14:1–2
Ps. 37:1–2
Ps. 90:5–6
Ps. 92:7
Ps. 103:15
Ps. 129:5–7
Isa. 37:27
Isa. 40:6–8
Isa. 51:12
1 Peter 1:24

Many Descendants

Job 5:25
Isa. 44:4
Isa. 66:14

Total Defeat

Num. 22:4

Discouragement

Ps. 102:4
Ps. 102:11

Humiliation

Dan. 4:25
Dan. 4:32–33
Dan. 5:21

God's Care

Matt. 6:30
Luke 12:28

Grasshoppers

Insignificance/Weakness

Num. 13:33
Isa. 40:22

Ruthless Invasion

Nahum 3:15

Grave

Evil Speech

Ps. 5:9
Rom. 3:13

Depth of God's Mysteries

Job 11:8

Hunger

Prov. 30:15–16
Isa. 5:14
Hab. 2:5

Weapons

Jer. 5:16

Abortion/Stillbirth

Jer. 20:17

Gentile Nations

Ezek. 37:12–13

Hypocrisy

Matt. 23:29
Luke 11:44

Gray Hair

Unrecognized Decay

Hosea 7:9

Crown

Prov. 16:31
Prov. 20:29

H

Hagar

The Old Covenant

Gal. 4:24–25

Hammer

Babylon

Jer. 50:23

Word of God

Jer. 23:29

Hand

Judgment (Heavy, Mighty)

Exod. 7:4–5
1 Sam. 5:6–7
1 Sam. 5:11
1 Sam. 6:3
1 Sam. 6:5
1 Sam. 7:13
1 Sam. 12:15
2 Sam. 24:17
Ps. 32:4
Isa. 1:25
Isa. 5:25
Isa. 9:12
Isa. 9:17
Isa. 9:21
Isa. 10:4
Isa. 14:27
Isa. 23:11
Isa. 26:11
Isa. 51:17
Jer. 25:17
Jer. 51:25
Lam. 2:3–4
Lam. 2:8
Lam. 3:3
Ezek. 6:14
Ezek. 13:9
Ezek. 14:9
Ezek. 14:13
Ezek. 16:27
Ezek. 35:3
Ezek. 39:21
Amos 1:8
Micah 5:9
Zeph. 1:4
Zeph. 2:13
Zech. 2:9

Affliction

Judg. 2:15
Ruth 1:13
Job 1:11
Job 2:5
Job 19:21
Job 23:2
Job 33:7
Ps. 38:2
Ps. 39:10
Acts 13:11

Victory

Gen. 49:8
Exod. 13:14
Exod. 13:16
Exod. 15:6
Exod. 15:12
Exod. 32:11
Deut. 2:15
Deut. 3:24
Deut. 4:34
Deut. 5:15
Deut. 6:21
Deut. 7:8
Deut. 7:19
Deut. 9:26
Deut. 11:2
Josh. 4:24
1 Kings 8:42
2 Chron. 6:32
2 Chron. 20:6
Ps. 44:2–4
Ps. 60:5
Ps. 89:18
Ps. 98:1
Ps. 108:6
Ps. 118:15–16
Ps. 136:12
Ps. 138:7
Ps. 144:7
Isa. 31:3
Isa. 41:20
Acts 4:30

Fulfillment/ Enablement

1 Kings 8:15
1 Kings 8:24
2 Chron. 6:15
2 Chron. 30:12
Ezra 7:6
Ezra 7:9
Ezra 7:28

Ezra 8:18
Ezra 8:22
Ezra 8:31
Neh. 2:8
Neh. 2:18
Ps. 18:35
Ps. 20:6
Ps. 37:24
Ps. 63:8
Ps. 89:21
Ps. 109:27
Ps. 139:5
Ps. 139:10
Isa. 41:10
Isa. 41:13
Ezek. 1:3
Ezek. 3:14
Ezek. 3:22
Ezek. 8:1
Ezek. 33:22
Ezek. 37:1
Ezek. 40:1
Dan. 10:10
Luke 1:66
Acts 11:21
1 Peter 5:6
Rev. 1:17

Mediation

Job 9:33

Righteousness

Ps. 48:10

Prosperity, Provision

Ps. 77:10
Ps. 104:28
Ps. 123:2
Ps. 145:16

God's Greatness

Isa. 40:12
Isa. 48:13
Isa. 66:2
Dan. 5:23
Hab. 3:4

Protection

Isa. 49:2
Isa. 51:16
John 10:28–29

Sovereignty (Right Hand)

Ps. 110:1
Jer. 18:6
Dan. 4:35
Matt. 22:44
Matt. 26:64
Mark 12:36
Mark 16:19
Luke 20:42
Acts 2:25
Acts 2:33–34
Acts 5:31
Acts 7:55–56
Rom. 8:34
Eph. 1:20
Col. 3:1
Heb. 1:3
Heb. 1:13
Heb. 8:1
Heb. 10:12
Heb. 12:2
1 Peter 3:22

Despair (Limp Hand)

Ezek. 7:17
Ezek. 21:7

Humility

Matt. 6:3

Spiritual Surgery

Matt. 5:30
Matt. 18:8
Mark 9:43

Fellowship

Gal. 2:9

Harlot

(see Prostitute/ Prostitution)

Harness

(see also Yoke)

Deceptive Tongue

Ps. 50:19

Harvest

(see also Plant)

Judgment

Job 24:24
Jer. 51:33
Hosea 6:11
Hosea 8:7
Hosea 10:13
Joel 3:13
Micah 4:12
Matt. 13:30
Matt. 13:39
Rev. 14:14–16

Good Works, Service

Isa. 5:2
Hosea 10:12
Matt. 13:8
Matt. 13:23
Mark 4:8
Mark 4:20
Luke 8:8
Luke 8:15
2 Cor. 9:10
Gal. 6:9
Heb. 6:7
Heb. 12:11
James 3:18

Converts

Matt. 9:37–38
Luke 10:2
John 4:36
Rom. 1:13

Financial Support

1 Cor. 9:7
2 Tim. 2:6

Death

Job 5:26
Job 24:24

Wise Words

Prov. 12:14
Prov. 18:20

Sin

Job 4:8

Head

Victory

Gen. 3:15
Deut. 28:13
Judg. 8:28

Death

Gen. 42:38
Gen. 44:29
Gen. 44:31
1 Kings 2:6
1 Kings 2:9

Blessings

Gen. 49:26
Deut. 33:16
Prov. 10:6

Dedication to God

Num. 6:5
Num. 6:7
Num. 6:9
Judg. 13:5
Judg. 16:17
1 Sam. 1:11

Defeat

Gen. 3:15
Deut. 28:44
1 Sam. 4:12
Rom. 16:20

Guilt

Josh. 2:19
2 Sam. 1:16
2 Sam. 3:29
1 Kings 2:33
1 Kings 2:37
1 Kings 8:32
Ezek. 18:13
Ezek. 33:4–5

Retribution

1 Sam. 25:39
Esther 9:25
Ps. 7:16
Prov. 25:22
Obad. 1:15
Rom. 12:20

Encouragement

Gen. 40:20
Ps. 3:3
Ps. 110:7
Luke 21:28

Shame

Job 10:15

Hills

Rev. 17:9

Healing

Forgiveness, Restoration

Ps. 41:4
Isa. 6:10
Isa. 30:26
Isa. 33:24
Isa. 53:5
Jer. 3:22
Jer. 17:14
Jer. 30:12
Jer. 30:17
Jer. 33:6
Jer. 44:11
Hosea 6:1
Hosea 14:4
Matt. 9:12
Mark 2:17
Luke 5:31
Heb. 12:13
1 Peter 2:24

Deliverance

Ps. 30:2
Ps. 107:20
Jer. 8:22
Jer. 14:19
Jer. 17:14
Jer. 51:8–9
Lam. 2:13
Hosea 5:13
Hosea 7:1
Nahum 3:19

Words of Encouragement

Prov. 12:18
Prov. 13:17
Prov. 15:4
Prov. 15:30
Prov. 16:24

Divine Comfort

Ps. 147:3

Heel

Treachery

Ps. 41:9
John 13:18

Satanic Attack

Gen. 3:15

Heifer

(see also Cows/Heifer)

Egypt

Jer. 46:20

Wife

Judg. 14:18

Babylon

Jer. 50:11

Stubbornness

Hosea 4:16

Captivity

Hosea 10:11

Helmet

Ephraim

Ps. 60:7
Ps. 108:8

Salvation

Isa. 59:17
Eph. 6:17
1 Thess. 5:8

Highway

(see also Road)

Deliverance

Isa. 11:16
Isa. 19:23
Isa. 35:8
Isa. 62:10

Consequences of Sin

Prov. 7:27

Personal Achievement

Prov. 15:19
Prov. 16:17

Coming of the King

Isa. 40:3

Hills

Joy

Ps. 65:12
Ps. 66:15
Ps. 114:4
Ps. 114:6
Isa. 55:12

Obstacles Removed

Isa. 41:15
Luke 3:5

Prosperity

Joel 3:18
Amos 9:13

Judgment

Nahum 1:5
Hab. 3:6

Honey

Prosperity/Wealth

Exod. 3:8
Exod. 3:17
Exod. 13:5
Exod. 33:3
Lev. 20:24
Num. 13:27
Num. 14:8
Num. 16:13–14
Deut. 6:3
Deut. 11:9
Deut. 26:9
Deut. 26:15
Deut. 27:3
Deut. 31:20
Deut. 32:13
Josh. 5:6
2 Kings 18:32
Job 20:17
Ps. 81:16
Jer. 11:5
Jer. 32:22
Ezek. 20:6
Ezek. 20:15

God's Word

Ps. 19:10
Ps. 119:103
Ezek. 3:3
Rev. 10:9–10

Temptation

Prov. 5:3

Praise/Honor

Prov. 25:16
Prov. 25:27

Human Love

Song of Sol. 4:11
Song of Sol. 5:1

Pleasant Words

Prov. 16:24

Hook

Conquest/Captivity (Hook in Nose)

2 Kings 19:28
2 Chron. 33:11
Job 41:2

Isa. 37:29
Ezek. 19:4
Ezek. 19:9
Ezek. 29:4
Ezek. 38:4
Amos 4:2
Hab. 1:15

Horns (Animal)

Victory

Deut. 33:17
Ps. 75:10
Jer. 48:25
Lam. 2:3
Lam. 2:17
1 Kings 22:11

Gentile Nations

Zech. 1:18–21

Power/Strength

1 Sam. 2:1
1 Sam. 2:10
1 Kings 22:11
Ps. 75:4–5
Ps. 75:10
Ps. 89:17
Ps. 89:24
Ps. 92:10
Ps. 112:9
Ezek. 29:21
Micah 4:13
Luke 1:69
Rev. 5:6

God

2 Sam. 22:3
Ps. 18:2

King/Dynasty

Ps. 132:17
Ps. 148:14
Dan. 7:8
Dan. 7:11
Dan. 7:20–21
Dan. 7:24
Dan. 8:3–9
Dan. 8:21–22
Rev. 12:3
Rev. 13:1
Rev. 17:3
Rev. 17:7
Rev. 17:12
Rev. 17:16

Messiah

Luke 1:69

Enemies

Ps. 22:21

Horses

Willfulness

Ps. 32:9
Prov. 26:3
Jer. 8:6

Stability

Isa. 63:13

Pride

Zech. 10:3

False Confidence

Ps. 20:7
Isa. 31:1

Testing

Jer. 12:5

Lewdness

Ezek. 23:20

Judgment

Rev. 6:1–8

Victory/Conquest

Rev. 19:11

House

The Glorified Body

2 Cor. 5:1

Jerusalem

Matt. 23:38
Luke 13:35

Heaven

John 14:2

The Human Body

Eccles. 12:3
Isa. 38:12
Matt. 12:29
Matt. 12:44
Luke 11:21
Luke 11:24–25

Land of Israel

Hosea 8:1
Hosea 9:15

The Tomb/Grave

Ps. 49:11

The Church

Eph. 2:19
1 Tim. 3:15
Heb. 3:6
Heb. 10:21
1 Peter 2:5

Hunter

Disaster

Ps. 140:11

Conquerors

Jer. 16:16

Freedom

Prov. 6:5

Social Chaos

Micah 7:2

Hurl

Judgment

Exod. 15:1
Exod. 15:4
Exod. 15:21
Neh. 9:11
Job 27:22
Jer. 22:26
Jer. 22:28
Lam. 2:1
Ezek. 32:4
Rev. 8:5
Rev. 8:7
Rev. 12:9–13

Salvation/Forgiven

Micah 7:19

Reproach

Ps. 79:12
Matt. 27:39
Mark 15:29
Luke 23:39
John 9:28
1 Peter 2:23

Husband

The Lord to Israel

Isa. 54:5
Jer. 3:14
Jer. 3:20
Jer. 31:32
Ezek. 16:32
Ezek. 16:45
Hosea 2:2
Hosea 2:7
Hosea 2:16

Chastened Israel

Isa. 54:1

Christ, to the Church

2 Cor. 11:2
Rev. 21:2

Hut

(see also Shelter)

Fragile Life

Job 27:18

God's Judgment

Isa. 24:20

Vulnerable

Isa. 1:8

I

Incense
(see Fragrance/ Incense)

Inheritance
(see also Lot [Inheritance], Treasure)

Wisdom

Eccles. 7:11

Sin's Consequences

Job 13:26
Prov. 11:29
Prov. 14:18

Honor

Prov. 3:35

God

Num. 18:20
Deut. 10:9
Deut. 18:2
Josh. 13:33
Ezek. 44:28

Israel

1 Sam. 26:19
2 Sam. 20:19
1 Kings 8:51
Ps. 28:9
Ps. 33:12
Ps. 68:9
Ps. 74:2
Ps. 78:62
Ps. 78:71
Ps. 94:5
Ps. 94:14
Isa. 19:25
Isa. 47:6
Isa. 63:17
Jer. 2:7
Jer. 10:16
Jer. 12:7–9
Micah 7:14
Micah 7:18

Nations

1 Kings 8:53
Ps. 2:8
Ps. 82:8

God's Will

Ps. 16:6

The Saints

Eph. 1:18

Iron

Build Character

Prov. 27:17

Drought

Lev. 26:19
Deut. 28:23

Security

Deut. 33:25

Strength

Job 40:18
Job 41:27
Ps. 107:16
Isa. 45:2
Dan. 2:33–45
Micah 4:13

Sovereignty

Ps. 2:9
Rev. 2:27
Rev. 12:5
Rev. 19:15

Stubbornness

Isa. 48:4
Jer. 6:28

Isaac

Children of Promise (God's Children)

Gal. 4:28

Ishmael

Children of Bondage (Legalism)

Gal. 4:28–31

J

Jewels

Lips Speaking Wisdom

Prov. 20:15

Babylon

Isa. 13:19

The Holy City

Rev. 21:11

Beautiful Eyes

Song of Sol. 5:12

Graceful Legs

Song of Sol. 7:1

The Jews

Exod. 28:21
Exod. 39:6–7
Exod. 39:14
Lam. 4:1
Ezek. 16:7
Zech. 9:16–17

K

Keys

Authority

Isa. 22:22
Matt. 16:19
Rev. 1:18
Rev. 3:7
Rev. 9:1
Rev. 20:1

The Fear of God

Isa. 33:6

False Interpretation

Luke 11:52

King/Reign

Distress

Job 15:24

Death

Job 18:14
Rom. 5:14
Rom. 5:17

Terror

Deut. 32:25

Believers

Rom. 5:17

Grace

Rom. 5:21

Sin

Rom. 5:21
Rom. 6:12

Kiss

Honest Answer

Prov. 24:26

Submission

Ps. 2:12

Reconciliation/God's Grace

Ps. 85:10

Knit/Weaving

Pregnancy

Job 10:11
Ps. 139:13
Ps. 139:15

Death

Isa. 38:12

Swiftness of Life

Job 7:6

L

Ladder
(see Stairway/Ladder)

Lamb
(see also Sheep/Flock)

Jesus Christ

Isa. 53:7
John 1:29
John 1:36
Acts 8:32
1 Cor. 5:7
1 Peter 1:19
Rev. 5:6
Rev. 5:8
Rev. 5:12–13
Rev. 6:1
Rev. 6:3
Rev. 6:5
Rev. 6:7
Rev. 6:16
Rev. 7:9–10
Rev. 7:14
Rev. 7:17
Rev. 12:11
Rev. 13:8
Rev. 14:1
Rev. 14:4
Rev. 14:10
Rev. 15:3
Rev. 17:14
Rev. 19:7
Rev. 19:9
Rev. 21:9
Rev. 21:14
Rev. 21:22
Rev. 21:23
Rev. 21:27
Rev. 22:1
Rev. 22:3

Bathsheba

2 Sam. 12:3–4

Innocent Victims

Isa. 53:7
Jer. 11:19

Believers—God's People

Isa. 40:11
Hosea 4:16
Luke 10:3
John 21:15

Peace

Isa. 11:6
Isa. 65:25

Victory

Ps. 114:4

Judgment

Jer. 51:40

Lamp

Readiness

Luke 12:35

The King (Dynasty)

2 Sam. 21:17
1 Kings 11:36
1 Kings 15:4
2 Kings 8:19
2 Chron. 21:7
Ps. 132:17

God

2 Sam. 22:29

Life

Job 18:5
Job 21:17
Ps. 18:28
Prov. 13:9
Prov. 20:20
Prov. 24:20

God's Blessing

Job 29:3

The Word

Ps. 119:105
Prov. 6:23

God's Knowledge/Searching

Prov. 20:27
Zeph. 1:12

Diligence

Prov. 31:18

Outlook/Conscience

Matt. 6:22–23
Luke 11:33–36

John the Baptist

John 5:35

Christ

Rev. 21:23

Holy Spirit

Rev. 4:5

Lampstand

Churches

Rev. 1:20
Rev. 2:5

Spiritual Provision

Zech. 4:1–6

God's Servants

Rev. 11:4

Leaf/Leaves

Weak Persons

Job 13:25
Isa. 1:30

Judgment

Isa. 34:4
Isa. 64:6

Spiritual Prosperity

Ps. 1:3
Prov. 11:28
Jer. 17:8

Legs

Man's Strength

Ps. 147:10

A Fool's Interpretation

Prov. 26:7

Shame and Disgrace

Isa. 7:20
Isa. 47:2

Leopard

The Impossible

Jer. 13:23

God's Judgment

Jer. 5:6
Hosea 13:7

Swift Movement

Hab. 1:8

Letter (Epistle)

The Saints/Spiritual Ministry

2 Cor. 3:2–3

Leviathan

Egypt

Ps. 74:14
Isa. 30:7
Isa. 51:9
Ezek. 29:3
Ezek 32:2

Any Evil Nation

Isa. 27:1

Light/Lamp

God

2 Sam. 22:29
Ps. 18:28
Ps. 27:1
Ps. 84:11
Isa. 60:19–20
Ezek. 1:4
Ezek. 1:27
Dan. 2:22
Micah 7:8
Mal. 4:2
1 Tim. 6:16
1 John 1:5
Rev. 21:23

Christ

Isa. 42:6
Isa. 49:6
Luke 2:32
John 1:1–9
John 8:12
John 9:5
Acts 13:47
Rev. 21:23

God's Word/Truth

Job 22:28
Ps. 19:8
Ps. 36:9
Ps. 43:3
Ps. 119:105
Ps. 119:130
Prov. 6:23
Isa. 5:20
Isa. 8:20
Titus 1:3
2 Peter 1:19

Life/Vitality

2 Sam. 22:29
Ezra 9:8
Job 3:20
Job 33:30
Ps. 13:3
Ps. 18:28
Ps. 38:10
Ps. 49:19
Ps. 56:13
John 1:4
2 Tim. 1:10

Death (Light Put Out)

Job 18:5–6
Job 18:18
Job 21:17
Prov. 13:9
Prov. 20:20
Prov. 24:20

God's Blessing

Job 30:26
Ps. 4:6
Ps. 44:3
Ps. 97:11
Ps. 112:4
Ps. 118:27
Prov. 4:18

God's People/Church

Matt. 5:14–16
Luke 16:8
John 5:35
Rom. 2:19
Eph. 5:8
1 Thess. 5:5
Rev. 1:12–13
Rev. 1:20
Rev. 2:1
Rev. 11:4

The Holy Spirit

Rev. 4:5

Salvation

Ps. 27:1
Isa. 9:2
Isa. 42:6
Isa. 49:6
Matt. 4:16
Luke 2:32
John 1:1–9
Acts 26:18
2 Cor. 4:6
Heb. 10:32
1 Peter 2:9
1 John 1:5–10
1 John 2:8–10

Israel

Isa. 49:6
Isa. 60:1–3

Satan

2 Cor. 11:14

Armor

Rom. 13:12

Godly Character

Ps. 89:15
Isa. 58:8
Matt. 6:22–23
Luke 11:34–36
John 3:19–21
2 Cor. 6:14
Eph. 5:8–14
1 John 1:5–10

King David

2 Sam. 21:17
1 Kings 11:36
1 Kings 15:4
2 Kings 8:19
2 Chron. 21:7
Ps. 132:17

Readiness

Luke 12:35

John the Baptist

John 5:35

Lightning

God's Judgment

Hosea 6:5
Hab. 3:11
Zech. 9:14

The Glorious Power of God

Ezek. 1:4
Ezek. 1:13–14
Rev. 4:5

Polished Swords

Ezek. 21:8–10
Ezek. 21:15
Ezek. 21:28

Face of the Son of Man

Dan. 10:6

Chariots

Nahum 2:4

Angel's Appearance

Matt. 28:3

Christ's Return

Matt. 24:27

Satan's Fall

Luke 10:18

Lily

The Beloved

Song of Sol. 2:1–2

Lips

Song of Sol. 5:13

Israel's Restoration

Hosea 14:5

Lion/Lioness

Israel

Num. 23:24
Num. 24:9
Jer. 12:8
Ezek. 19:1–9
Hosea 10:1

Hosea 14:7
Micah 5:8

Christ

Rev. 5:5

Jerusalem

Isa. 29:1

Tribe of Judah

Gen. 49:9

Tribe of Gad

Deut. 33:20

Anger

Prov. 19:12
Prov. 20:2

Courage

2 Sam. 1:23
2 Sam. 17:10
1 Chron. 12:8
Prov. 28:1

Excuses

Prov. 22:13
Prov. 26:13

God

Job 10:16
Isa. 31:4
Isa. 38:13
Jer. 2:30
Jer. 25:30
Jer. 25:38
Jer. 49:19
Jer. 50:44
Lam. 3:10
Hosea 5:14
Hosea 11:10
Hosea 13:7–8
Joel 3:16
Amos 1:2

Enemies

Ps. 7:2
Ps. 10:9
Ps. 17:12
Ps. 22:13
Ps. 22:21
Ps. 35:17
Ps. 57:4
Ps. 58:6
Ps. 91:13
Isa. 5:29
Jer. 2:15

Evil Rulers

Prov. 28:15
Ezek. 22:25
Zeph. 3:3
Rev. 13:2

Babylon

Jer. 4:7
Jer. 51:38
Dan. 7:4

Angelic Creatures

Ezek. 1:10
Ezek. 10:14
Rev. 4:7

Egypt

Ezek. 32:2

Satan

1 Peter 5:8

Loud Shout

Rev. 10:3

Peace

Isa. 11:7
Isa. 65:25

Locust

Rejection

Ps. 109:23

Strength

Job 39:20

Army

Judg. 6:5
Judg. 7:12
Jer. 46:23
Jer. 51:14
Jer. 51:27

Judgment

Isa. 33:4
Jer. 51:14
Jer. 51:27

Restoration

Joel 2:25

Multiplication

Nahum 3:15–16

Robbery

Nahum 3:16

Abandoning Responsibility

Nahum 3:17

Lot (Inheritance)

Man's Providential Place in Life

Job 31:2
Ps. 16:5
Prov. 16:33
Eccles. 3:22
Eccles. 5:18–19
Eccles. 9:9

Judgment

Ps. 11:6
Prov. 6:33
Isa. 17:14
Jer. 13:24–25

Association (By Choice)

Ps. 50:18
Prov. 1:14
Isa. 57:6

M

Maggot
(see Worm/Maggot)

Manure
(see also Offal, Refuse, Scum)

Humiliation

Isa. 25:10–11
Nahum 3:6

Marriage/ Engagement

Israel's Restoration

Isa. 62:3–5
Hosea 2:19

God's Covenant Relationship with Israel

Isa. 54:5
Jer. 3:14

God's Covenant Relationship with the Church

2 Cor. 11:2
Eph. 5:22–33
Rev. 19:7–8

Mask

Pretense/Greed

1 Thess. 2:5

Measuring Line
(see Plumb Line/ Measuring Line)

Meat

People of Israel

Ezek. 11:3
Ezek. 11:7
Ezek. 24:4
Ezek. 24:10

Victims of Evil Leaders

Micah 3:3

Medicine
(see also Physician)

The Word

Ps. 107:20

Cheerful Heart

Prov. 17:22

Forgiveness/Hope

Jer. 8:22

Melchizedek

A Type of Christ

Gen. 14:17–20
Ps. 110:4
Heb. 5:6
Heb. 5:10
Heb. 6:20
Heb. 7:1–3

Melting

Fear/Discouragement

Exod. 15:15
Josh. 2:9
Josh. 2:11
Josh. 2:24
Josh. 7:5
Josh. 14:8
Ps. 107:26
Isa. 13:7
Isa. 19:1
Ezek. 21:7
Ezek. 21:15
Nahum 2:10

Divine Power

Ps. 46:6
Ps. 68:2
Ps. 97:5
Amos 9:5
Micah 1:4
Nahum 1:5

Suffering

Ps. 22:14

Punishment

Ezek. 22:20–22
Ezek. 24:9–12

Victory

1 Sam. 14:16
Isa. 14:31

Menstruation
(see Lev. 15:19–30)

Uncleanness
Ezek. 36:17

Rejection
Isa. 30:22

Self-Righteousness
Isa. 64:6

Milk

Spiritual Food for the Immature
1 Cor. 3:1–2
Heb. 5:12–13
1 Peter 2:2

Prosperity, Abundance
Exod. 3:8
Exod. 3:17
Exod. 13:5
Exod. 33:3
Lev. 20:24
Num. 13:27
Num. 14:8
Num. 16:13–14
Deut. 6:3
Deut. 11:9
Deut. 26:9
Deut. 26:15
Deut. 27:3
Deut. 31:20
Josh. 5:6
Job 20:17
Job 29:6
Isa. 60:16
Jer. 11:5
Jer. 32:22
Ezek. 20:6
Ezek. 20:15
Joel 3:18

Human Conception
Job 10:10

Stirring Up Anger
Prov. 30:33

God's Grace
Isa. 55:1

Material Support for Ministry
1 Cor. 9:7

Mirror

Revelation of Character
Prov. 27:19

God's Law
2 Cor. 3:18
James 1:23–25

The Sky
Job 37:18

Mist/Vapor
(see also Clouds)

Wealth Gained by Lies
Prov. 21:6

Forgiveness
Isa. 44:22

Unfaithful Love
Hosea 6:4

Sinners
Hosea 13:3

Life
James 4:14

Monster
(see Leviathan)

Mortar

Weakness, Defenseless
Isa. 41:25

Moth

Man's Weakness
Job 4:19
Job 13:28

Impermanence of Wealth
Job 27:18
Ps. 39:11
Matt. 6:19–20
Luke 12:33
James 5:2

Divine Judgment
Isa. 50:9
Isa. 51:8
Hosea 5:12

Mother

A City
2 Sam. 20:19

A Leader
Judg. 5:7

Decay/Death
Job 17:14

Obedient Saints
Matt. 12:47–49
Mark 3:33–35
Luke 8:21

Loving Concern

Isa. 49:15
Isa. 66:13
Rom. 16:13
1 Thess. 2:7

Heavenly Jerusalem

Gal. 4:26

Prosperity

Isa. 49:23

Mountain/Hill

Security

Ps. 30:7
Ps. 97:5
Ps. 125:2

Hopelessness

Job. 14:18–19

A Kingdom

Jer. 51:25
Dan. 2:35
Dan. 2:44–45

Obstacles

Isa. 40:4
Isa. 41:15
Isa. 45:2
Isa. 49:11
Zech. 4:7
Matt. 17:20–21
Mark 11:23
Luke 3:5
1 Cor. 13:2

Divine Judgment/ Power

Isa. 64:1
Isa. 64:3
Micah 1:4
Nahum 1:5
Hab. 3:10
Rev. 8:8

God's Righteousness

Ps. 36:6

Joy

Ps. 98:8
Ps. 114:4–6
Isa. 44:23
Isa. 49:13
Isa. 55:12

Prosperity

Joel 3:18
Amos 9:13

Mouth/Swallow

Earth Receiving Something/Judgment

Gen. 4:11
Num. 16:30
Num. 16:32
Num. 16:34
Num. 26:10
Deut. 11:6

Destruction of a City

2 Sam. 20:19

Defeat

2 Sam. 17:16
Ps. 35:25
Ps. 124:3
Isa. 28:4
Jer. 51:34
Jer. 51:44
Hosea 8:7
Hab. 1:13

Work of Evil Doers

Prov. 1:12

Victory Over Death

Isa. 25:8
1 Cor. 15:54

Lack of Perspective

Matt. 23:24

Divine Wrath

Exod. 7:12
Exod. 15:12
Job 37:20
Ps. 21:9
Ps. 106:17
Lam. 2:2
Lam. 2:5
Lam. 2:16

Resurrection

2 Cor. 5:4

Mud/Mire

Ignominious Defeat

2 Sam. 22:42
Ps. 18:42
Isa. 10:6
Zech. 10:5

Chastening

Job 30:19

Despair

Ps. 40:2

Compromise

Prov. 25:26

Mule

(see Donkey)

N

Nails

Wise Words

Eccles. 12:11

Nakedness

(see also Clothing)

Innocence

Gen. 2:25

Shame/Punishment

Gen. 3:7
Gen. 3:10–11
Gen. 9:20–21
Isa. 47:3
Lam. 1:8
Nahum 3:5
Rev. 17:16

Poverty

Job 1:21
Eccles. 5:15
1 Tim. 6:7

Mourning

Micah 1:8

Spiritual Poverty

Rev. 3:17–18

Nest

Security

Num. 24:21
Job 39:27
Jer. 48:28
Jer. 49:16
Ezek. 17:23
Ezek. 31:6
Dan. 4:21
Obad. 1:4
Hab. 2:9

Disturbance

Deut. 32:11
Isa. 16:2

Straying

Prov. 27:8

Net

God's Chastening

Job 19:6

Death (Inevitable)

Job 18:8

Judgment

Ps. 9:15
Ps. 35:8
Ps. 141:10
Isa. 51:20
Lam. 1:13
Ezek. 12:13
Ezek. 17:20
Ezek. 19:8
Ezek. 32:3
Hosea 7:12

Evil Plots (Being Trapped)/Injustice

Ps. 10:9
Ps. 35:7
Ps. 57:6
Ps. 140:4
Hosea 5:1
Micah 7:2

Flattery

Prov. 29:5

Evil Times

Eccles. 9:12

Military Prowess

Hab. 1:15–17

Kingdom of Heaven

Matt. 13:47

Nursing

(see also Mother)

Sharing Jerusalem's Blessing

Isa. 66:11–12

Spiritual Care

Num. 11:12

Kingdom Blessings

Isa. 49:23
Isa. 60:16

O

Offal
(see also Manure, Refuse, Scum)

Humiliation

Nahum 3:6
Mal. 2:3

Oil

Gladness

Ps. 45:7
Isa. 61:3
Heb. 1:9

Prosperity

Deut. 32:13
Deut. 33:24

Lying Words

Ps. 55:21
Prov. 5:3

Unity

Ps. 133:2

Rebuke

Ps. 141:5

Failure

Prov. 27:16

Holy Spirit

Zech. 4:6
Zech. 4:12

Victory

Ps. 92:10

Olive Shoots/ Olive Trees

Children

Ps. 128:3

Wicked Man

Job 15:33

Godly Man

Ps. 52:8

Judgment

Isa. 17:6
Isa. 24:13

Israel

Isa. 17:6
Jer. 11:16
Hosea 14:6
Rom. 11:17–24

Witnesses/Leaders

Zech. 4:3
Zech. 4:11–12
Rev. 11:4

Gentile Believers

Rom. 11:17
Rom. 11:24

Oven
(see also Furnace)

Suffering

Lam. 5:10

Lust

Hosea 7:4
Hosea 7:6–7

Ox/Oxen

Conquest

Num. 22:4

Strength/Power

Num. 23:22
Num. 24:8
Deut. 33:17
Ps. 22:21
Ps. 92:10

Joy

Ps. 29:6

Ignorance

Prov. 7:22

Instinct

Isa. 1:3

Peace/Harmony

Isa. 11:7
Isa. 65:25

Angelic Creatures

Ezek. 1:10
Rev. 4:7

P

Pasture

The Lord

Jer. 50:7

The Promised Land

Ps. 74:1
Ps. 79:13
Ps. 95:7
Ps. 100:3
Jer. 23:1
Jer. 23:3
Jer. 25:36–38
Jer. 49:20
Jer. 50:19
Ezek. 34:31

Salvation

John 10:9

Path

Way of Life (Good or Evil)

Num. 22:32
2 Sam. 22:37
Neh. 9:19
Job 13:27
Job 18:10
Job 22:15
Job 29:6
Job 33:11
Ps. 16:11
Ps. 17:5
Ps. 18:36
Ps. 23:3
Ps. 25:4
Ps. 44:18
Ps. 77:19
Ps. 119:32
Ps. 119:35
Ps. 119:101
Ps. 119:104–5
Ps. 119:128
Isa. 2:3
Isa. 41:3
Micah 4:2
Luke 1:79
Acts 2:28
2 Cor. 6:3
Heb. 12:13

Security/Safety

Ps. 27:11
Prov. 3:6
Prov. 3:17
Prov. 4:11
Prov. 4:18
Prov. 4:26
Prov. 12:28
Prov. 23:19
Isa. 26:7
Isa. 43:16
Jer. 31:9

Judgment

Job 19:8
Ps. 35:6
Ps. 78:50
Prov. 10:9
Prov. 22:5
Jer. 23:12
Lam. 3:9
Hosea 9:8
Hosea 13:7

Danger

Job 24:13
Ps. 57:6
Ps. 140:5
Ps. 142:3
Prov. 1:15
Prov. 2:9
Prov. 2:13
Prov. 2:15
Prov. 2:18–20
Prov. 4:14
Prov. 5:6
Prov. 5:8
Prov. 7:25
Prov. 15:10
Prov. 15:19
Prov. 15:24
Prov. 16:29
Prov. 28:10
Isa. 3:12
Isa. 30:11
Hosea 2:6

Understanding

Prov. 21:16
Isa. 40:14

Hard Heart

Matt. 13:4
Mark 4:4
Mark 4:15
Mark 13:19

Luke 8:5
Luke 8:12

Sea Lanes

Ps. 8:8

Justice (Injustice)

Prov. 8:20
Isa. 59:8

Tradition

Jer. 6:16
Jer. 18:15

Spiritual Preparation

Isa. 40:3
Matt. 3:3
Mark 1:3
Luke 3:4

God's Ways

Rom. 11:33

Pearls

(see also Jewels)

Spiritual Truth

Matt. 7:6

Kingdom of Heaven

Matt. 13:45

Pebbles

Hail

Ps. 147:17

Peg/Firm Place

New Beginning

Ezra 9:8

Leaders

Isa. 22:23

Pen (for Writing)

The Tongue

Ps. 45:1

Physician

Useless Friends

Job 13:4

False Prophets

Jer. 8:22

Jesus

Matt. 9:12
Mark 2:17
Luke 5:31

Pig

Ineffective Sacrifice

Isa. 66:3

Lack of Discretion/ Discernment

Prov. 11:22
Matt. 7:6

Apostasy

2 Peter 2:22

Pillars

Daughters

Ps. 144:12

Stability of Earth

Ps. 75:3

Wisdom

Prov. 9:1

Christian Leaders

Gal. 2:9

Overcomers

Rev. 3:12

God's Servant

Jer. 1:18

Church

1 Tim. 3:15

Pit/Plunge

Adulteress/Prostitute

Prov. 22:14
Prov. 23:27

Chastening

Job 9:31
Ps. 88:6

Retribution

Ps. 7:15
Ps. 9:15
Ps. 35:8
Ps. 94:13
Ps. 140:10
Prov. 26:27
Ezek. 19:4
Ezek. 19:8

Threats/Danger

Ps. 35:7
Ps. 57:6
Jer. 18:20
Jer. 18:22

Salvation/Deliverance

Ps. 40:2
Ps. 103:4
Jonah 2:6

Chance

Eccles. 10:8

Exile

Zech. 9:11

Sin

Hosea 9:9
1 Peter 4:4

Ruin

1 Tim. 6:9

Plank

Major Fault

Matt. 7:3–5
Luke 6:41–42

Plant

(see also Flower)

Establish a Nation (especially Israel)

Exod. 15:17
2 Sam. 7:10
1 Chron. 17:9
Ps. 44:2
Ps. 80:8
Ps. 80:15
Isa. 5:2
Isa. 60:21
Isa. 61:3
Jer. 2:21
Jer. 11:17
Jer. 18:9
Jer. 24:6
Jer. 31:27–28
Jer. 32:41
Jer. 42:10
Ezek. 19:10–13
Hosea 2:23
Amos 9:15

Unbelievers/False Doctrine

Matt. 15:13

Burial of a Corpse

1 Cor. 15:37

Fruitfulness

Ps. 1:3
Ps. 92:13
Jer. 17:8

Rulers

Isa. 40:23–24

The Wicked

Job 5:3
Job 8:16–19
Jer. 12:1–2

Captivity

Ezek. 17:4–8

Retribution

Job 4:8
Hosea 10:12–13

Ministry

1 Cor. 3:6
James 1:21

Plow

Persecution

Ps. 129:3

Sinners

Job 4:8

Discipline

Hosea 10:11

Loyalty

Luke 9:62

Deception/Unfairness

Judg. 14:18

Judgment

Ps. 141:7
Jer. 26:18
Micah 3:12

Prosperity

Ezek. 36:9
Amos 9:13

Financial Support

1 Cor. 9:10

War

Joel 3:10

Peace

Micah 4:3

God's Wisdom and Grace

Isa. 28:23–24

Repentance

Jer. 4:3
Hosea 10:12

Plumb Line/ Measuring Line

God's Judgment

2 Kings 21:13
Isa. 34:11
Lam. 2:8
Amos 7:7–8

God's Righteousness

Isa. 28:17

Completed Work

Zech. 4:10

Vastness of Creation

Job 38:5

Promise of Restoration

Jer. 31:39
Zech. 1:16
Zech. 2:1–4

Pot

Jerusalem

Ezek. 11:3
Ezek. 11:7
Ezek. 11:11
Ezek. 24:3

Ezek. 24:6
Ezek. 24:11

Leviathan's Breath

Job 41:20

Leviathan's Swimming

Job 41:31

Foolish Laughter

Eccles. 7:6

Babylon

Jer. 1:13

Restoration

Jer. 18:4

Judgment

Jer. 19:10–11

Rejection

Jer. 22:28

Potsherd/Pottery (Broken)

Weakness

Ps. 22:15

Man (Humility)

Isa. 45:9

Rejection

Ps. 31:12

Judgment

Ps. 2:9
Isa. 30:14
Jer. 25:34
Rev. 2:27

Potter

(see also Clay)

Human Conception

Job 10:8

God

Isa. 29:16
Isa. 45:9
Isa. 64:8
Jer. 18:6
Rom. 9:21

Cyrus

Isa. 41:25

Pouring

Conception

Job 10:10

Anger (Words)

Job 15:13
Ps. 94:4

Service

2 Kings 3:11

God's Revelation

Ps. 19:2
Prov. 1:23

Wrath of God

2 Chron. 12:7
2 Chron. 34:21
2 Chron 34:25
Ps. 69:24
Ps. 79:6
Isa. 42:25
Jer. 1:14
Jer. 7:20
Jer. 10:25
Jer. 14:16
Jer. 44:6
Jer. 48:12
Jer. 48:18
Lam. 2:4
Lam. 4:11
Ezek. 7:8
Ezek. 14:19
Ezek. 20:8
Ezek. 20:13
Ezek. 20:21
Ezek. 20:33
Ezek. 22:22
Ezek. 30:15
Ezek. 36:18
Hosea 5:10
Nahum 1:6
Zeph. 3:8
Rev. 14:10
Rev. 16:1

Blessing

Mal. 3:10
Luke 6:38

Defeat

Ps. 18:42

The Holy Spirit

Isa. 32:15
Isa. 44:3
Ezek. 39:29
Joel 2:28–29
Zech. 12:10
Acts 2:17–18
Acts 2:33
Acts 10:45
Titus 3:6

Consecration/Worship

Gen. 28:18
Gen. 35:14
Lev. 8:12
Lev. 21:10
1 Sam. 7:6
2 Sam. 23:16
1 Chron. 11:18

Repentance

1 Sam. 7:6

Prayer/Anguish

1 Sam. 1:15
Job 3:24
Ps. 42:4

Ps. 62:8
Ps. 102:1
Ps. 142:2
Lam. 2:11
Lam. 2:19

Death

Ps. 22:14
Isa. 53:12
Matt. 26:28
Mark 14:24
Luke 22:20
Phil. 2:17
2 Tim. 4:6

Contempt

Job 12:21
Ps. 107:40

Deceiving Speech

Prov. 6:19
Prov. 14:5
Prov. 19:5
Prov. 19:9

Wicked Deeds

Jer. 6:7

Pregnancy/ Conception/Birth

Gen. 4:1

Despair

Num. 11:12

Sinners/Sin

Job 15:35
Ps. 7:14
Isa. 33:11
Isa. 59:4
Isa. 59:13
James 1:13–15

Disappointment/ Failure

2 Kings 19:3
Isa. 26:17–18
Isa. 33:11
Hosea 9:11
Hosea 13:13

Nations "Born"

Isa. 66:7–9

Salvation (New Birth)

John 1:13
John 3:3–8
1 Cor. 15:8
James 1:18
1 Peter 1:3
1 Peter 1:23
1 John 2:29
1 John 3:9
1 John 4:17
1 John 5:1
1 John 5:4
1 John 5:18

Resurrection

Isa. 26:19

Prisoner

Bondage to Sin/Law

Luke 4:18
Rom. 7:23
Gal. 3:22–23

Prostitute/ Prostitution

Idolatry

Exod. 34:15–16
Lev. 17:7
Lev. 19:29
Lev. 20:5–6
Num. 15:39
Deut. 31:16
Judg. 2:17
Judg. 8:27
Judg. 8:33
1 Chron. 5:25
2 Chron. 21:11
2 Chron 21:13
Ps. 106:39
Isa. 57:5–8
Jer. 2:20
Jer. 3:1–3
Jer. 13:25–27
Ezek. 16:15
Ezek. 16:28
Ezek. 16:30–35
Ezek. 23:3–18
Ezek. 23:27
Ezek. 23:29
Ezek. 23:35
Ezek. 23:43–44
Hosea 4:12
Hosea 5:3–4
Hosea 6:10

Evil World System

Rev. 17:1
Rev. 17:5
Rev. 17:15–16
Rev. 19:2

Ninevah

Nahum 3:4

Jerusalem

Isa. 1:21

Q

Quarry

Abraham

Isa. 51:1

R

Rags

Self -Righteousness

Isa. 64:6

Rain

(see also Storms)

God's Blessing

Exod. 16:4

Ezek. 34:26

Hosea 6:3

God's Word

Deut. 32:2

Isa. 55:10

The King/Godly Leaders

Ps. 72:6

The King's Favor

Prov. 16:15

Physical Blows

Job 20:23

Wise Words

Job 29:23

Israel

Micah 5:7

Ungodly Rulers

Prov. 28:3

Divine Judgment

Isa. 28:2

Divine Righteousness

Isa. 45:8

Hosea 10:12

Quarrelsome Wife

Prov. 27:15

Misplaced Honor

Prov. 26:1

Rainbow

Sign at God's Covenant with Noah

Gen. 9:12–17

Glory of God's Throne

Ezek. 1:28

Rev. 4:3

Halo of a Mighty Angel

Rev. 10:1

Rampart

Salvation

Isa. 26:1

God's Faithfulness

Ps. 91:4

Razor

Destructive Tongue

Ps. 52:2
Ps. 57:4
Ps. 59:7

Assyrian King

Isa. 7:20

Reap

(see Harvest)

Reed

Weakness

1 Kings 14:15
2 Kings 18:21
Ezek. 29:6–7
Matt. 11:7
Luke 7:24

Egypt

2 Kings 18:21
Isa. 36:6
Ezek. 29:6–7

God's Enemies

Isa. 42:3
Matt. 12:20

Bowing the Head

Isa. 58:5

Refine

Faithful Prophet

Jer. 6:27–30

God's Chastening/ Testing

Ps. 12:6
Ps. 66:10
Isa. 48:10
Jer. 6:29
Jer. 9:7
Dan. 11:35
Dan. 12:10
Zech. 13:9
Mal. 3:2–3
1 Peter 1:7

True Wealth

Rev. 3:18

Refuge

Lies

Isa. 28:15
Isa. 28:17

God

Deut. 33:27
2 Sam. 22:3
2 Sam. 22:31
Ps. 2:12
Ps. 5:11
Ps. 7:1
Ps. 9:9
Ps. 11:1
Ps. 14:6
Ps. 16:1
Ps. 17:7
Ps. 18:2
Ps. 18:30
Ps. 25:20
Ps. 31:1–2
Ps. 31:4
Ps. 31:19
Ps. 34:8
Ps. 34:22
Ps. 36:7
Ps. 37:40
Ps. 46:1
Ps. 57:1
Ps. 59:16
Ps. 61:3–4
Ps. 62:7–8
Ps. 64:10
Ps. 71:1
Ps. 71:3
Ps. 71:7
Ps. 73:28
Ps. 91:2
Ps. 91:4
Ps. 91:9
Ps. 94:22
Ps. 118:8–9
Ps. 119:114
Ps. 141:8
Ps. 142:5
Ps. 144:2
Prov. 30:5
Isa. 25:4
Isa. 27:5
Isa. 57:13
Jer. 16:19
Jer. 17:17
Joel 3:16
Nahum 1:7

God's Way

Prov. 10:9

Fear of the Lord

Prov. 14:26

God's Glory

Isa. 4:6

Zion

Isa. 14:32

Godly Leaders

Isa. 32:2

Refuse

(see also Manure, Offal, Scum)

Shame, Humiliation

2 Kings 9:37
Ps. 83:10
Isa. 5:25
Isa. 25:10
Jer. 8:2
Jer. 9:22
Jer. 16:4
Jer. 25:33
Lam. 3:45
1 Cor. 4:13

Register/Book/Writing

Citizenship

Ps. 87:4–6
Dan. 12:1
Luke 10:20
Heb. 12:23

God's Recognition/Reward

Mal. 3:16
Rev. 3:12

God's Sovereign Will

Ps. 139:16

Salvation

Phil. 4:3
Rev. 3:5
Rev. 13:8
Rev. 17:8
Rev. 20:12
Rev. 20:15
Rev. 21:27

Judgment

Jer. 17:13
Dan. 7:10
Rev. 20:12

Ministry of Grace

Prov. 3:3
Prov. 7:3
Jer. 31:33
2 Cor. 3:2–3
Heb. 8:10
Heb. 10:16

Reins/Bit/Bridle

Control

Ps. 32:9
James 1:26
James 3:3

Judgment

2 Kings 19:28
Isa. 30:28
Isa. 37:29

Riches

God's Word

Ps. 119:14

Spiritual Blessing

Isa. 55:2
Rom. 2:4
Rom. 9:23
Rom. 11:12
Rom. 11:33
Eph. 1:7
Eph. 1:18
Eph. 2:7
Eph. 3:8
Eph. 3:16
Phil. 4:19
Col. 1:27
Col. 2:2
Col. 3:16

Ring

God's Judgment

Jer. 22:24

Lack of Discretion

Prov. 11:22

Forgiveness/Sonship

Luke 15:22

River

Discouragement

Job 14:19

Rejecting God

Isa. 8:5–8
Jer. 2:18
Jer. 17:13

God's Blessing

Job 20:17
Ps. 36:8
Ps. 46:4

Peace

Isa. 48:18
Isa. 66:12

Grief

Lam. 2:18

Justice

Amos 5:24

Satanic Opposition

Rev. 12:15–16

Joy

Ps. 98:8

Trials

Isa. 43:2

Egypt

Jer. 46:7–8

Road

(see also Highway)

Suffering

Job 30:13
Lam. 1:4

Deliverance

Isa. 49:11
Isa. 57:14
Luke 3:5

Way to Destruction (Broad)

Matt. 7:13

Way to Life (Narrow)

Matt. 7:14

Deception

Isa. 59:8

Robbery/Robbers

Death

Isa. 38:10

Selfishness

Mal. 3:8–9

Fierce Fighting

2 Sam. 17:8

Judgment

Hosea 13:8

False Shepherd

John 10:1
John 10:8

Hypocrites

Jer. 7:11
Matt. 21:13
Mark 11:17
Luke 19:46

Rock/Stone

God

Gen. 49:24
Deut. 32:4
Deut. 32:15
Deut. 32:18
Deut. 32:30–31
1 Sam. 2:2
2 Sam. 22:2–3
2 Sam. 22:32
2 Sam. 22:47
2 Sam. 23:3
Ps. 18:2
Ps. 18:31
Ps. 18:46
Ps. 19:14
Ps. 28:1
Ps. 31:2–3
Ps. 42:9
Ps. 62:2
Ps. 62:6–7
Ps. 71:3
Ps. 78:20
Ps. 89:26
Ps. 92:15
Ps. 94:22
Ps. 95:1
Ps. 144:1
Isa. 17:10
Isa. 26:4
Isa. 30:29
Isa. 33:6
Isa. 44:8
Hab. 1:12

Messiah

Exod. 17:6
Num. 20:8–11
Deut. 8:15
Ps. 118:22
Isa. 8:14
Isa. 28:16
Dan. 2:34–35
Dan. 2:45
Matt. 21:42–44
Mark 12:10
Luke 20:17–18
Acts 4:11
Rom. 9:32–33
1 Cor. 10:4
1 Peter 2:6–8

False Gods

Deut. 32:31
Deut. 32:37

Hopelessness

Job 14:18

Prosperity

Job 29:6

Hardness

Job 6:12
Job 38:30
Job 41:24
Jer. 5:3
Ezek. 3:9
Ezek. 11:19
Ezek. 36:26

Security

Num. 24:21
Ps. 27:5

Ps. 31:2
Ps. 40:2
Ps. 61:2
Isa. 32:2
Jer. 49:16
Obad. 1:3

Intimate Meetings

Exod. 33:21–22
Song of Sol. 2:14

Abraham

Isa. 51:1

Jerusalem

Zech. 12:3

Obedience (Build on Rock)

Matt. 7:24–25
Luke 6:48

Peter's Confession

Matt. 13:5
Matt. 13:20
Matt. 16:18

Hard Heart

Ezek. 11:19
Ezek. 36:26
Mark 4:5
Mark 4:16
Luke 8:6
Luke 8:13

Sinking/Weight

Exod. 15:5
Neh. 9:11

Silence

Exod. 15:16

Honor Wasted

Prov. 26:8

Believers

1 Peter 2:5

Provocation by a Fool

Prov. 27:3

Rod

(see also Club/Rod)

Assyria

Isa. 10:5
Isa. 10:24
Isa. 14:29

Chastening

Job 9:34
Job 21:9
Ps. 89:32
Prov. 10:13
Prov. 13:24
Prov. 14:3
Prov. 22:15
Prov. 23:13–14
Prov. 26:3
Prov. 29:15
Isa. 30:32
Lam. 3:1
Micah 6:9

Human Oppression

Prov. 22:8
Isa. 9:4
Isa. 10:5
Isa. 11:5
Micah 5:1

God's Word

Isa. 11:4

Impending Judgment

Ezek. 7:10–11

Babylon

Isa. 14:5

Roll

Retribution

Prov. 26:27

Judgment

Isa. 22:18
Isa. 34:4
Jer. 51:25
Heb. 1:12
Rev. 6:14

Justice

Amos 5:24

New Beginning

Josh. 5:9

Death

Isa. 38:12

Suffering

Job 30:14

Root

(see also Plant, Trees, Uproot)

Death

Job 18:16
Isa. 40:24

Evil Person

Deut. 29:18
Heb. 12:15

Reviving (Take Root)

2 Kings 19:30
Isa. 27:6
Isa. 37:31
Hosea 14:5

Being Established

Job 5:3
Eph. 3:17
Col. 2:7

Cause of Trouble

Deut. 29:18
Job 19:28
1 Tim. 6:10

Israel

Ps. 80:9
Ps. 80:15
Rom. 11:16–18

Prosperity

Prov. 12:12
Jer. 12:2

Messiah

Isa. 11:1
Isa. 11:10
Isa. 53:2
Rom. 15:12
Rev. 5:5
Rev. 22:16

Judgment

Isa. 40:24
Hosea 9:16
Amos 2:9
Matt. 3:10
Matt. 13:29
Matt. 15:13
Luke 3:9

Spiritual Deficiency

Matt. 13:6
Matt. 13:21
Mark 4:6
Mark 4:17
Luke 8:13

Security

Prov. 10:30
Prov. 12:3

Rose

The Beloved

Song of Sol. 2:1

Rottenness

Name of Wicked

Prov. 10:7

God's Judgment

Hosea 5:12
James 5:2

Envy

Prov. 14:30

Ruby

(see also Jewels)

Wisdom

Job. 28:18
Prov. 3:15
Prov. 8:11

Faithful Wife

Prov. 31:10

God's Restoration of Jerusalem

Isa. 54:12

Rulers

Lam. 4:7

Run/Runner/Race

Swiftness of Life

Job 9:25

Challenges of Life

Jer. 12:5

Cowardice (Run Away)

Neh. 6:11
Jer. 17:16
John 10:5
John 10:12–13

The Sun

Ps. 19:5

Life/Ministry

Acts 20:24
1 Cor. 9:24
1 Cor. 9:26
Gal. 2:2
Gal. 5:7
Phil. 2:16
Phil. 3:12–14
2 Tim. 4:7
Heb. 12:1

Sin

Jer. 2:23

The Word

Ps. 147:15

Abandoning Truth

2 John 1:9

S

Sacrifices/Offering

Judgment

Isa. 34:6
Jer. 46:10
Jer. 50:27
Ezek. 39:17–19
Zeph. 1:7–8

Humility

Ps. 51:17

Human Body

Rom. 12:1

Praise

Heb. 13:15–16

Good Works and Sharing

Heb. 13:15–16

Jewish People

Isa. 66:20

Worship/Prayer

Ps. 141:2

Foolish Vows

Eccles. 5:2

Material Gifts

Phil. 4:18

Salt

A Covenant Sign

Lev. 2:13
Num. 18:19
2 Chron. 13:5
Ezek. 43:24

Judgment

Gen. 19:26
Deut. 29:23
Judg. 9:45
Jer. 48:9

Believers

Matt. 5:13

Character

Mark 9:50
Luke 14:34

Pure Speech

Col. 4:6
James 3:11–12

Trials

Mark 9:49

Sand

Israel (Numerous as)

Gen. 22:17
Gen. 32:12
2 Sam. 17:11
1 Kings 4:20
Isa. 10:22
Isa. 48:19
Hosea 1:10
Rom. 9:27
Heb. 11:12

Grain

Gen. 41:49

Soldiers (Armies)

Josh. 11:4
Judg. 7:12
1 Sam. 13:5
Rev. 20:8

Wisdom

1 Kings 4:29
Ps. 139:18

Misery

Job 6:2–3

Long Life

Job 29:18

Food (Birds)

Ps. 78:27

Widows

Jer. 15:8

Ministers

Jer. 33:22

Prisoners

Hab. 1:9

Sandals

Claim Possession

Ruth 4:7–8
Ps. 60:8
Ps. 108:9

Humility (Remove Sandal)

Exod. 3:5
Josh. 5:15
Isa. 20:2
Matt. 3:11
Mark 1:7
Luke 3:16
John 1:27
Acts 7:33
Acts 13:25

Readiness

Exod. 12:11

Forgiveness/ Acceptance

Luke 15:22

Sarah

New Covenant

Gal. 4:24–26

Exemplary Wife

1 Peter 3:1–6

Sawdust

Minor Fault

Matt. 7:3
Luke 6:41

Scarecrow

Idols

Jer. 10:5

Scepter

Judah

Gen. 49:10
Ps. 60:7
Ps. 108:8
Ezek. 21:10
Ezek. 21:13

Messiah

Num. 24:17

Just Rule

Ps. 2:9
Ps. 45:6
Ps. 110:2
Heb. 1:8
Rev. 2:27
Rev. 12:5
Rev. 19:15

Unjust Rule

Ps. 125:3

Judgment (Broken Scepter)

Isa. 14:5
Isa. 30:31
Jer. 48:17
Amos 1:5
Amos 1:8
Zech. 10:11

Babylon

Isa. 14:5

Scroll

Judgment

Isa. 34:4
Zech. 5:1–4
Rev. 6:14

Scum

(see also Manure, Offal, Refuse)

Humiliation

Lam. 3:45
1 Cor. 4:13

Sea

Knowledge of God

Isa. 11:9

Nations

Isa. 17:12–13
Isa. 60:5
Jer. 51:42
Ezek. 26:3
Dan. 7:2–3
Luke 21:25
Rev. 13:1
Rev. 17:15

Abundance of Righteousness

Isa. 48:18

The Wicked

Isa. 57:20
Jude 1:13

Restlessness/Trouble

Jer. 49:23

Discipline/Suffering

Lam. 2:13

Forgiveness

Micah 7:19

Glory of God

Hab. 2:14

Doubt

James 1:6

Seal/Signet

The Dawn

Job 38:14

Devotion

Song of Sol. 8:6

Acceptance/Approval

Jer. 22:24
Hag. 2:23
John 6:27
1 Cor. 9:2

Ownership

2 Cor. 1:22
Eph. 1:13
Eph. 4:30
2 Tim. 2:19

Judgment (Reserved)

Deut. 32:34

Forgiveness

Job 14:17

Virginity

Song of Sol. 4:12

Spiritual Blindness

Isa. 29:10

Seat/Throne

Leaders

Isa. 22:23
Matt. 23:2

Humiliation

Luke 14:9

Judgment

Rom. 14:10
2 Cor. 5:10

Honor

1 Sam. 2:8
Ps. 113:8

Pride

Matt. 23:6
Mark 12:39
Luke 11:43
Luke 20:46

Seed/Sowing

The Word of God

Mark 4:14
Luke 8:11
1 Cor. 3:6
1 Cor. 9:11
2 Cor. 9:10
1 Peter 1:23

The Kingdom of Heaven

Matt. 13:31
Mark 4:31
Luke 13:19

Faith

Matt. 17:20

Scattered Saints

Acts 8:1
Acts 8:4
Acts 11:19
James 1:1
1 Peter 1:1

Children of the Kingdom

Matt. 13:24
Matt. 13:38

Children of the Evil One

Matt. 13:25
Matt. 13:38

Dead Body

1 Cor. 15:37–38
1 Cor. 15:42–44

Money Given to Others

Ps. 112:9
2 Cor. 9:6–10

The Divine Nature in the Believer

1 John 3:9

Rulers

Isa. 40:23–24

Christ (in Death and Resurrection)

John 12:23–25

Lifestyle

Prov. 11:18
Prov. 22:8
Hosea 8:7
Hosea 10:12
Gal. 6:7–10
James 3:18

Service

John 4:37
1 Cor. 9:11
Gal. 6:9–10

Selling

Defeat Before Enemy (Enslavement)

Deut. 32:30
Judg. 2:14

Judg. 3:8
Judg. 4:2
Judg. 10:7
1 Sam. 12:9
Esther 7:4
Ps. 44:12
Isa. 50:1
Isa. 52:3
Joel 3:6–7

Abandonment to Evil

1 Kings 21:20
1 Kings 21:25
2 Kings 17:17
Prov. 23:23
Hosea 8:9–10

Slavery of Sin

Rom. 7:14

Salvation

Isa. 55:1–2

False Ministry

2 Cor. 2:17

Serpent/Dragon

Satan

Gen. 3:1–4
Gen. 3:13–14
2 Cor. 11:3
Rev. 12:9
Rev. 12:15
Rev. 20:2

Tribe of Dan

Gen. 49:17

Victory (Tread on the Serpent)

Ps. 91:13

False Confidence

Isa. 14:29

Nation (Egypt) in Retreat

Jer. 46:22

Nebuchadnezzar

Jer. 51:34

Servant

(see Slave/Hired Servant)

Shadows/Shade

Disappointment

Isa. 30:2
Isa. 59:9

Care/Protection

Judg. 9:15
Ps. 17:8
Ps. 36:7
Ps. 57:1
Ps. 63:7
Ps. 91:1
Ps. 121:5
Isa. 4:6
Isa. 25:4
Isa. 32:1
Isa. 49:2
Isa. 51:16
Lam. 4:20
Ezek. 17:23
Ezek. 31:6
Ezek. 31:12
Ezek. 31:17

Communion

Song of Sol. 2:3

Physical Decay

Job 16:16
Job 17:7

OT Law

Col. 2:17
Heb. 8:5
Heb. 10:1

Changeableness

James 1:17

Brevity of Life

1 Chron. 29:15
Job 8:9
Job 14:2
Ps. 102:11
Ps. 109:23
Ps. 144:4
Eccles. 6:12
Eccles. 8:13

Death

Job 3:5
Job 10:21–22
Job 38:17
Ps. 23:4
Isa. 9:2
Matt. 4:16
Luke 1:79

Sheaves

(see also Harvest)

Death

Job 5:26

Family of Jacob

Gen. 37:7

Divine Judgment

Micah 4:12

Sheep/Flock
(see also Lamb)

God's People (Israel, Church)

Num. 27:17
2 Sam. 24:17
1 Kings 22:17
1 Chron. 21:17
2 Chron. 18:16
Ps. 74:1
Ps. 77:20
Ps. 78:52
Ps. 79:13
Ps. 80:1
Ps. 95:7
Ps. 100:3
Ps. 119:176
Isa. 13:14
Isa. 40:11
Isa. 63:11
Jer. 13:17
Jer. 13:20
Jer. 23:1–3
Jer. 25:35–36
Jer. 31:10
Jer. 50:6
Jer. 50:17
Ezek. 34:1–13
Ezek. 34:15–22
Ezek. 34:31
Ezek. 36:37
Micah 2:12
Micah 7:14
Zech. 9:16
Zech. 10:2
Zech. 13:7
Matt. 9:36
Matt. 10:6
Matt. 15:24
Matt. 25:32
Matt. 26:31
Mark 6:34
Luke 12:32
John 10:1–4
John 10:7–8
John 10:11–16
John 10:26–27
John 21:16–17
Acts 20:28
Rom. 8:36
1 Cor. 9:7
Heb. 13:20
1 Peter 5:2

Disobedient Sinners

Ps. 49:14
Isa. 53:6
Jer. 12:3
1 Peter 2:25

Teeth

Song of Sol. 4:2
Song of Sol. 6:6

Messiah

Isa. 53:7
Acts 8:32

God's Servants

Matt. 10:16
Matt. 26:31
Mark 14:27

Family

Job 21:11
Ps. 107:41

Persecution

Ps. 44:11
Ps. 44:22
Rom. 8:36

Shelter

Wisdom

Eccles. 7:12

Money

Eccles. 7:12

Tabernacle

Ps. 27:5
Ps. 31:20
Ps. 61:4
Ps. 91:1

Israel

Isa. 1:8

The Lord

Isa. 25:4

Godly Leaders

Isa. 32:2

Shepherd

God

Gen. 48:15
Gen. 49:24
Ps. 23:1
Ps. 28:9
Ps. 80:1
Isa. 40:11
Jer. 31:10
Eccles. 12:11

Messiah/Jesus

Ezek. 34:16
Ezek. 34:23
Micah 5:4
Zech. 13:7
Matt. 2:6
Matt. 26:31
Mark 14:27
John 10:11–16

Heb. 13:20
1 Peter 2:25
1 Peter 5:4
Rev. 7:17

Kings, Rulers

Num. 27:17
2 Sam. 5:2
2 Sam. 7:7
1 Kings 22:17
1 Chron. 11:2
1 Chron. 17:6
2 Chron. 18:16
Ps. 78:71
Isa. 13:14
Isa. 44:28
Isa. 63:11
Jer. 3:15
Jer. 10:21
Jer. 12:10
Jer. 22:22
Jer. 23:1–4
Jer. 25:34–35
Jer. 50:6
Ezek. 34:1–10
Zech. 11:3–17
Zech. 13:7
Matt. 9:36
Mark 6:34
Jude 1:12

Spiritual Leaders

Jer. 17:16
Acts 20:28
Eph. 4:11
1 Peter 5:2

Shield

God as Protector

Gen. 15:1
Deut. 33:29
2 Sam. 22:3
2 Sam. 22:31
Ps. 3:3
Ps. 7:10
Ps. 18:2
Ps. 18:30
Ps. 28:7
Ps. 33:20
Ps. 59:11
Ps. 84:11
Ps. 115:9–11
Ps. 119:114
Ps. 144:2
Prov. 2:7
Prov. 30:5

Israel's King

Ps. 84:9
Ps. 89:18

God's Faithfulness (Truth)

Ps. 91:4

Faith

Eph. 6:16

Shiloh

Messiah

Gen. 49:10

God's Judgment/ Rejection

Ps. 78:60
Jer. 7:12–15
Jer. 26:6–9

Ship/Shipwreck/ Drift

Faithful Wife

Prov. 31:14

The Tongue (Rudder)

James 3:4

Apostasy

1 Tim. 1:19

Decayed Nation

Isa. 33:23

Tyre

Ezek. 27:1–36

Spiritual Decay

Heb. 2:1

Shoots

(see also Stump)

Messiah

Isa. 11:1
Isa. 53:2
Ezek. 17:22

Israel

Ps. 80:11
Isa. 60:21
Hosea 14:6

King Jehoiachin

Ezek. 17:4

Gentile Believers

Rom. 11:17

Helpless People

2 Kings 19:26
Isa. 37:27

Children

Ps. 128:3

Moab

Isa. 16:8

God's Judgment

Isa. 18:5

Shroud

Universal Death

Isa. 25:7

Shut Up
(see also Floodgates)

Judgment/Chastening

Deut. 11:17
1 Kings 8:35
2 Chron. 6:26
2 Chron. 7:13

Stillbirth

Job 3:10

Last Opportunity

Isa. 22:22
Matt. 23:13
Matt. 25:10
Rev. 3:7–8

Sieve/Sift/ Winnow

Judgment

Isa. 30:28
Jer. 15:7
Amos 9:9

Separating People

Judg. 7:4

Temptation

Luke 22:31

Silver/Treasure

Wisdom

Prov. 2:4
Prov. 3:14
Prov. 8:10
Prov. 8:19
Prov. 16:16

God's Word

Ps. 12:6
Ps. 119:72

Refining/Chastening

Ps. 66:10
Prov. 17:3
Isa. 48:10
Zech. 13:9
Mal. 3:3

Righteous Tongue

Prov. 10:20

Good Name

Prov. 22:1

Spiritual Decay

Isa. 1:22
Jer. 6:30
Ezek. 22:18

Singing/Song

Careless Hearing of the Word

Ezek. 33:31–32

The Lord

Exod. 15:2
Ps. 118:14
Isa. 12:2

Humiliation

Ps. 69:12
Lam. 3:14
Lam. 3:63

Encouragement

Job 35:10
Ps. 77:6

Protection

Ps. 32:7

Sink
(see also Drown/Sink)

Fear

Gen. 42:28
Josh. 2:11
Josh. 5:1
Josh. 7:5

Failure

Deut. 28:43

Suffering

Ps. 69:2
Ps. 69:14

Judgment

Exod. 15:5
Exod. 15:10
Jer. 51:64

Earthquake

Amos 8:8

Sleep

Acts 20:9

Despair

Song of Sol. 5:6

Skirts

Shame

Isa. 47:2
Jer. 13:22
Jer. 13:26
Nahum 3:5

Defilement

Lam. 1:9

Slave/Hired Servant

Babylonian Exile

Isa. 40:2

Life (Difficult)

Job 7:1–2
Job 14:6
Job 14:14

Sleep

Natural Death

Gen. 15:15
Gen. 47:30
Deut. 31:16
1 Kings 1:21
1 Kings 2:10
1 Kings 11:43
1 Kings 14:20
1 Kings 14:31
1 Kings 15:8
1 Kings 15:24
1 Kings 16:6
1 Kings 16:28
1 Kings 22:40
1 Kings 22:50
2 Kings 8:24
2 Kings 9:28
2 Kings 10:35
2 Kings 13:9
2 Kings 13:13
2 Kings 14:16
2 Kings 14:22
2 Kings 14:29
2 Kings 15:7
2 Kings 15:22
2 Kings 15:38
2 Kings 16:20
2 Kings 20:21
2 Kings 21:18
2 Kings 22:20
2 Kings 24:6
2 Chron. 9:31
2 Chron. 12:16
2 Chron. 14:1
2 Chron. 16:13
2 Chron. 21:1
2 Chron. 26:2
2 Chron. 26:23
2 Chron. 27:9
2 Chron. 28:27
Job 3:13
Ps. 7:5
Ps. 13:3
Ps. 49:19
Ps. 76:5
Ps. 90:5
Jer. 51:39
Jer. 51:57
Dan. 12:13
Matt. 9:24
Mark 5:39
Luke 8:52
John 11:11
Acts 7:60
Acts 13:36
1 Cor. 11:30
1 Cor. 15:6
1 Cor. 15:18
1 Cor. 15:20
1 Cor. 15:51
1 Thess. 4:13–15
1 Thess. 5:10

Spiritual Stupor

Isa. 29:10
Eph. 5:14
1 Thess. 5:6

God's Seeming Inaction (see Awaken)

Ps. 44:23
Ps. 78:65

Impending Judgment

2 Peter 2:3

Sling Out

(see also Hurl)

Judgment

Exod. 15:1
Exod. 15:4
Exod. 15:21
1 Sam. 25:29
Neh. 9:11
Isa. 22:17
Jer. 10:18
Jer. 22:26
Jer. 22:28
Ezek. 32:4
Jonah 2:3

Forgiveness

Micah 7:19

Insult (Reproach)

1 Sam. 25:14
Ps. 22:7
Ps. 79:12
Lam. 2:1
Matt. 27:39
Mark 15:29
Luke 23:39
John 9:28
1 Peter 2:23

Stupidity

Prov. 26:8

Slug

Judgment

Ps. 58:8

Smoke
(see also Furnace)

Divine Judgment/ Anger
Gen. 19:28
Exod. 19:18
2 Sam. 22:9
Ps. 18:8
Ps. 21:9
Ps. 74:1
Ps. 80:4
Isa. 30:27
Isa. 34:10
Isa. 51:6
Hosea 13:3
Rev. 14:11
Rev. 19:3

Fate of the Wicked
Ps. 37:20
Ps. 68:2

Transiency of Life
Ps. 102:3

Sluggard
Prov. 10:26

Invading Army
Isa. 14:31

Hypocrites
Isa. 65:5

Snake
(see Serpent/Dragon)

Snares/Trap

Moses
Exod. 10:7

Idols
Exod. 23:33
Deut. 7:16
Judg. 2:3
Judg. 8:27
Ps. 106:36

The Ungodly
Exod. 34:12
Josh. 23:13
Judg. 2:3
Prov. 7:23
Eccles. 7:26
Jer. 5:26
Hosea 5:1

A Woman
1 Sam. 18:21
Eccles. 7:26

Causes of Sin or Trouble
Ps. 25:15
Ps. 31:4
Ps. 69:22
Ps. 91:3
Ps. 119:110
Ps. 140:5
Ps. 141:9
Ps. 142:3
Prov. 22:5
Prov. 28:10
Hosea 9:8
Rom. 11:9

Wrong Words
Prov. 18:7

Illegal Riches
Prov. 21:6

Fear of Man
Prov. 29:25

Unknown Future
Eccles. 9:12
Luke 21:34

God
Isa. 8:14

Sin
Prov. 29:6

Death
2 Sam. 22:6
Ps. 18:5
Prov. 13:14
Prov. 14:27

Rash Words
Prov. 20:25

Temptation
1 Tim. 3:7
1 Tim. 6:9
2 Tim. 2:26

Snow

Dependability (Cool)
Prov. 25:13

Leprous (White)
Exod. 4:6
Num. 12:10
2 Kings 5:27

Cleansing
Ps. 51:7
Isa. 1:18

Victory
Ps. 68:14

Honor for a Fool
Prov. 26:1

Word of God
Isa. 55:10

Leaders

Lam. 4:7

Glory/Holiness

Dan. 7:9
Matt. 28:3
Rev. 1:14

Snuff Out

Judgment

Job 18:5
Job 21:17
Prov. 13:9
Prov. 20:20
Prov. 24:20
Isa. 42:3
Isa. 43:17
Ezek. 32:7
Matt. 12:20

Sodom and Gomorrah

Total Destruction

Deut. 29:23
Isa. 1:9
Isa. 13:19
Jer. 49:18
Jer. 50:40
Lam. 4:6
Amos 4:11
Zeph. 2:9
Rom. 9:29

Extreme Wickedness

Isa. 3:9
Jer. 23:14

Witnesses Against Unbelief

Matt 10:15
Matt. 11:23–24
Luke 10:12

Rescue of the Godly

2 Peter 2:6–7

Eternal Judgment

Jude 1:7

Jerusalem

Rev. 11:8

Soil/Field

The Human Heart

Matt. 13:4–5
Matt. 13:8
Matt. 13:19
Mark 4:5
Mark 4:8
Mark 4:20
Luke 8:8
Luke 8:15

The World

Matt. 13:38
Luke 10:2

The Local Church

1 Cor. 3:9

An Assigned Area of Ministry

2 Cor. 10:13
1 Peter 5:3

Soldier/Warrior

(see also Army)

God

Exod. 15:3
Job 15:33
Isa. 42:13
Jer. 14:9
Jer. 20:11

Locusts

Joel 2:7

A Carefree Attitude

Micah 2:8

Financial Support

1 Cor. 9:7

Servant of God

Phil. 2:25
2 Tim. 2:3–4
Philem. 1:2

Sow/Sowing

(see Seed/Sowing)

Spears

Evil Speech

Ps. 57:4

Spend

Sacrificial Service

Isa. 49:4
Isa. 58:10
2 Cor. 12:15

Wasted Effort

Isa. 55:2

God's Wrath

Ezek. 5:13
Ezek. 6:12
Ezek. 7:8
Ezek. 13:15
Ezek. 20:8
Ezek. 20:21

Spoils

Christ's Victory on the Cross

Isa. 53:12

God's Word

Ps. 119:162

Defeat

Jer. 30:16

Springs/Well/Wellspring

(see Water/Well [for Drinking])

The Human Heart

Prov. 4:23

Adultery

Prov. 5:15–16

False Teachers

2 Peter 2:17

Spiritual Satisfaction

John 4:14
Rev. 7:17
Rev. 21:6

Security

Deut. 33:28
Hosea 13:15

A Compromiser

Prov. 25:26

The Bride

Song of Sol. 4:12

God's People

Isa. 58:11

God

Jer. 2:13
Jer. 17:13

Stairway/Ladder

Link Between Heaven and Earth

Gen. 28:12

Christ

John 1:51

Stars

Christ

Num. 24:17
Rev. 22:16

King of Babylon (a Symbol of Satan)

Isa. 14:12

Return of Christ

2 Peter 1:19
Rev. 2:28

Satan

Isa. 14:12
Rev. 8:10–11
Rev. 9:1
Rev. 9:11

An Army (Host)

Judg. 5:20
2 Kings 17:16
2 Kings 21:3
2 Kings 21:5
2 Kings 23:4–5
Neh. 9:6
Ps. 33:6
Isa. 34:4
Isa. 40:26
Isa. 45:12
Jer. 19:13
Zeph. 1:5

False Teachers

Jude 1:13

God's People

Song of Sol. 6:10
Dan. 8:10
Dan. 12:3
Phil. 2:15

Israel

Gen. 15:5
Gen. 22:17
Gen. 26:4
Gen. 37:9
Exod. 32:13
Deut. 1:10
Deut. 10:22
Deut. 28:62
1 Chron. 27:23
Neh. 9:23

Angels

Job 38:7
Isa. 14:13
Rev. 8:12
Rev. 12:4

God's Servants

Rev. 1:16
Rev. 1:20
Rev. 2:1
Rev. 3:1

Stench

(see also Fragrance/Incense)

A Bad Reputation (Name)

Gen. 34:30
Exod. 5:21
1 Sam. 13:4
1 Sam. 27:12
2 Sam. 10:6
1 Chron. 19:6

Judgment

Isa. 3:24
Isa. 34:3

Joel 2:20
Amos 4:10

Folly

Eccles. 10:1

Steward

Of the Faith/Word

Rom. 3:2
Rom. 6:17
1 Cor. 4:1–2
1 Cor. 9:17
1 Cor. 16:13
Gal. 2:7
1 Thess. 2:4
1 Tim. 1:11
1 Tim. 1:18–19
1 Tim. 6:20
2 Tim. 1:13–14
2 Tim. 2:2
Titus 1:3
Titus 1:7
1 Peter 5:3
Jude 1:3

Of Ministry Opportunity

Matt. 25:14–30
Luke 12:42–48

Stick

Dryness

Lam. 4:8

Salvation

Amos 4:11
Zech. 3:2

Stillborn Child

Judgment

Ps. 58:8

Sting

Sin

1 Cor. 15:55

Rebuke

Ezek. 5:15

Stone

(see Rock/Stone)

Store Up

Remember the Word

Prov. 2:1
Prov. 7:1

God's Plans

Job 23:14
Isa. 2:12

Victory

Prov. 2:7

Knowledge

Prov. 10:14

The Lord's Salvation

Isa. 33:6

Sin

Hosea 13:12

The Heart

Matt. 12:35
Luke 6:45

Hope

Col. 1:5

Judgment

Job 21:19

Storms

(see also Rain)

God's Chastening/ Judgment

Job 9:17
Job 27:20
Job 30:22
Ps. 50:3
Ps. 83:15
Prov. 1:27
Prov. 10:25
Isa. 29:6
Jer. 11:16
Jer. 23:19
Jer. 25:32
Jer. 30:23

The Ruthless

Isa. 25:4

Trials of Life

Ps. 55:8
Isa. 4:6
Isa. 25:4
Isa. 32:2

Advancing Army

Judg. 9:52
Ezek. 38:9
Dan. 11:40
Nahum 2:4
Hab. 3:14

False Teachers

2 Peter 2:17

Stranger
(see also Alien)

False Shepherds
John 10:5

God
Jer. 14:8

God's People
1 Chron. 29:15
Ps. 39:12
Ps. 119:19
Heb. 11:13
1 Peter 1:1
1 Peter 1:17
1 Peter 2:11

Jesus
Matt. 25:35
Matt. 25:38
Matt. 25:43–44

Straw

Futility
Isa. 33:11

The Wicked
Job 21:18

Strength
Job 41:27
Job 41:29

Divine Judgment
Isa. 5:24

Peace
Isa. 11:7
Isa. 65:25

Humiliation
Isa. 25:10

False Prophecy
Jer. 23:28

Human Wisdom
1 Cor. 3:12

Streams
(see also River)

Undependable Friends
Job 6:14–17

Nations
Isa. 2:2
Isa. 66:12
Jer. 51:44
Micah 4:1

Judgment
Isa. 30:33

Righteousness
Amos 5:24

Wealth
Job 29:6

God's Blessing
Ps. 46:4
Ps. 65:9
Ps. 126:4

Tears
Ps. 119:136
Jer. 9:18
Lam. 3:48

Sexual Sin
Prov. 5:16

Leaders
Isa. 32:2

Holy Spirit
John 7:38

Street

Humiliation
2 Sam. 22:43
Ps. 18:42
Isa. 10:6
Isa. 51:23
Micah 7:10

Deception
Isa. 59:14

Joy
Zech. 8:5

Wealth
Zech. 9:3

Stronghold
(see also Fortress, Rock/Stone)

God
2 Sam. 22:3
Ps. 9:9
Ps. 18:2
Ps. 27:1
Ps. 37:39
Ps. 43:2
Ps. 52:7
Ps. 144:2
Joel 3:16

Stubble

Astrologers, Stargazers
Isa. 47:14

Invading Locusts
Joel 2:5

Judgment
Obad. 1:18
Nahum 1:10

Sinners
Mal. 4:1

Stumble/ Stumbling Block

Obstruction
Matt. 16:23
Rom. 14:13
2 Cor. 6:3

The Cross
1 Cor. 1:23

Christ
Rom. 9:32–33

Israel's Unbelief
Rom. 11:9–10

Abuse of Freedom
1 Cor. 8:9

Stump

Hope
Job 14:7–8

Jewish Remnant
Isa. 6:13

Davids' Family
Isa. 11:1

Humiliation
Dan. 4:15
Dan. 4:23
Dan. 4:26

Sun/Dawning

God
Ps. 84:11
Mal. 4:2

A Bridegroom
Ps. 19:4–5

A Champion
Ps. 19:4–5

Vindication, Justice
Ps. 37:6
Isa. 58:8
Isa. 62:1

Permanence
Ps. 72:5
Ps. 72:17
Ps. 89:36

The Lover (Christ?)
Song of Sol. 6:10

God's People
Matt. 13:43

Path of the Just
Prov. 4:18

Clothing
Rev. 12:1

Eyes of the Leviathan
Job 41:18

God's Glory
Matt. 17:2
Acts 26:13
Rev. 1:16
Rev. 10:1

An Army
Joel 2:2

Salvation
Ps. 27:1
Isa. 9:2
Matt. 4:16
Luke 1:77–79

Encouragement
Ps. 112:4

Return of Christ
2 Peter 1:19

Truth
Isa. 8:20

Swallow
(see Eating/ Devouring/ Swallowing)

Sweat

Labor
Gen. 3:19

Blood Like Sweat
Luke 22:44

Sweep (Away)

Judgment, Disaster
Gen. 18:23–24
Gen. 19:15
Gen. 19:17
Exod. 14:27
Num. 16:26
Judg. 5:21
1 Sam. 12:25
1 Chron. 21:12
Job 1:17
Job 1:19
Job 5:13
Job 21:18
Job 27:2
Ps. 58:9
Ps. 73:19
Ps. 136:15
Prov. 1:27

Prov. 10:25
Isa. 8:8
Isa. 11:15
Isa. 14:23
Isa. 28:19
Dan. 2:35
Dan. 11:22
Dan. 11:26
Hosea 4:19
Micah 7:2
Hab. 1:6
Hab. 1:11
Zeph. 1:2–3
Zeph. 2:2

Death

Ps. 90:5

Forgiveness

Isa. 44:22

Injustice

Prov. 13:23

Sins

Isa. 64:6

Satanic Opposition

Rev. 12:4
Rev. 12:15

Invasion

Isa. 21:1

Trials

Ps. 42:7
Ps. 88:16
Ps. 124:4–5
Jonah 2:3

Self-Reformation

Matt. 12:44
Luke 11:25

Sword

(see also Devour, Eating/Devouring/ Swallowing)

Divine Discipline

Lev. 26:25
2 Sam. 12:10
1 Chron. 21:12
1 Chron. 21:16
1 Chron. 21:27
Hosea 6:5

Danger

Exod. 5:21

Impending Judgment

Deut. 32:41
Ps. 7:12
Ezek. 21:9–11

Sharp Tongue or Words

Job 5:15
Ps. 55:21
Ps. 57:4
Ps. 59:7
Ps. 64:3
Prov. 30:14

Consequences of Sin

Prov. 5:4

God's Word

Isa. 49:2
Hosea 6:5
Eph. 6:17
Heb. 4:12
Rev. 1:16
Rev. 2:12
Rev. 2:16

Conflict

Matt. 10:34

Pain of Heart

Luke 2:35

Civil Authority

Rom. 13:4

False Testimony, Lies

Prov. 25:18

God

Deut. 33:29

T

Tablet

The Human Heart

Deut. 6:6
Prov. 3:3
Prov. 7:3
Jer. 17:1
2 Cor. 3:3

Tail

Lying Prophets

Isa. 9:14–15

Victory

Deut. 28:13

Defeat

Deut. 28:44

Leaders

Isa. 19:15

Target

Suffering/ Discipline

Job 7:20
Job 16:12
Lam. 3:12

Taste

Experiencing God

Ps. 34:8
Heb. 6:4–5
1 Peter 2:3

Enjoying the Word

Ps. 119:103
Ezek. 3:3
Rev. 10:10

Experiencing Death

Matt. 16:28
Mark 9:1
Luke 9:27
John 8:52
Heb. 2:9

Tearing/Ripping/ Rending

Judgment

1 Sam. 15:27–28
1 Sam. 24:4
1 Sam. 28:17
1 Kings 11:11–13
1 Kings 11:30–31
1 Kings 14:8
2 Kings 17:21
Job 19:10
Ps. 50:22
Ps. 52:5
Jer. 18:7
Hosea 5:14
Hosea 6:1

Sorrow/Repentance

Joel 2:13

God's Presence

Isa. 64:1

Spiritual Discipline/ Suffering

Job 19:10
2 Cor. 13:10

Anger/Violence

Job 18:4
Ps. 7:2
Isa. 7:6

Leaving Friends

Acts 21:1
Col. 3:17
1 Thess. 2:17

Death

Job 18:14

Inner Conflict

Phil. 1:23

Tears/Weeping

Food of Sorrow

Ps. 42:3
Ps. 80:5
Ps. 102:9

Stream/Fountain/Flood

Job 16:20
Ps. 6:6
Ps. 119:136
Jer. 9:1
Jer. 9:18
Lam. 1:16

Lam. 2:18
Lam. 3:48
Mal. 2:13

Punishment

Matt. 13:42
Matt. 13:50
Matt. 22:13
Matt. 24:51
Matt. 25:30
Luke 13:28

Teeth/Fangs

(see also Tooth)

Attacks of the Wicked

Job 29:17
Ps. 3:7
Ps. 35:16
Ps. 37:12
Ps. 57:4
Ps. 58:6
Ps. 112:10
Ps. 124:6
Prov. 30:14
Lam. 2:16

God's Chastening

Job 16:9

Strength

Isa. 41:15

Responsibility

Jer. 31:29–30
Ezek. 18:1–2

Punishment

Matt. 8:12
Matt. 13:42
Matt. 13:50
Matt. 22:13
Matt. 24:51
Matt. 25:30
Luke 13:28

Temperature

Spiritual Indifference

Rev. 3:15–16

Spiritual Passion

Luke 24:32

Spiritual Insensitivity

Matt. 24:12

Anger

Exod. 11:8
Ps. 39:3
Prov. 15:18
Prov. 19:19
Prov. 22:24
Prov. 29:22
Ezek. 38:18

Temple

Christ's Body

John 2:19–21

The Church Local

1 Cor. 3:9
1 Cor. 3:16–17
Rom. 15:20

The Believer's Body

1 Cor. 6:19–20
2 Cor. 6:16

The Church Universal

Eph. 2:21

Glorified Body

2 Cor. 5:1

Tent

Human Body

2 Cor. 5:1
2 Cor. 5:4
2 Peter 1:13

David's Dynasty

Amos 9:11
Acts 15:15–16

Death

Job 4:21
Job 18:6
Job 18:14
Isa. 38:12
2 Cor. 5:1
2 Peter 1:13–14

God's Judgment

Job 19:12
Job 20:26
Ps. 52:5
Ps. 69:25
Jer. 10:20

God's Protection

Rev. 7:15

The Heavens

Ps. 19:4
Ps. 104:2
Isa. 40:22

Pilgrim Life

Heb. 11:9

Prosperity/Security

Job 5:24
Ps. 61:4
Ps. 91:10
Prov. 14:11
Isa. 33:20
Isa. 54:2
Jer. 30:18

Christ (Like a Tent Peg)

Zech. 10:4

Thief

Thoughtless Person

Prov. 25:20

Sinner

Job 24:14

Disgrace

Jer. 2:26

Satan

John 10:10

Return of Christ

Matt. 24:43
Luke 12:39
1 Thess. 5:2
1 Thess. 5:4
2 Peter 3:10
Rev. 3:3
Rev. 16:15

Invading Locusts

Joel 2:9

Death

Jer. 9:21

Thirst

Desire for God

Ps. 42:2
Ps. 63:1
Ps. 143:6
Matt. 5:6
Rev. 22:17

Unfulfilled Desire

Isa. 29:8

Vengeance

Jer. 46:10

Spiritual Satisfaction

Isa. 44:3
Isa. 55:1
John 4:13–14
John 6:35
John 7:37
Rev. 21:6

Thistle

A King of Judah

2 Kings 14:9–10
2 Kings 14:18–19

Thorns

Judgment

Gen. 3:18
Isa. 5:6
Isa. 7:23–25
Isa. 10:17
Jer. 12:13
Hosea 9:6
Hosea 10:8
Nahum 1:10

Trouble/Temptation

Num. 33:55
Josh 23:13
Judg. 2:3

Evil People

2 Sam. 23:6
Ezek. 2:6
Ezek. 28:24

Death

Ps. 118:12

Obstacles

Prov. 15:19
Prov. 22:5

Foolish Laughter

Eccles. 7:6

Enemy Army

Isa. 27:4

Unrepentant Heart

Jer. 4:3
Matt. 13:7
Matt. 13:22
Mark 4:7
Mark 4:18
Luke 8:7
Luke 8:14
Heb. 6:8

Suffering

2 Cor. 12:7

Threshing/ Threshing Floor

Defeat

2 Kings 13:7

Removing Evil

Prov. 20:26

Affliction/Violence

Isa. 21:10
Amos 1:3

Enablement

Isa. 41:15
Micah 4:13

Judgment

Ps. 1:4
Isa. 27:12
Jer. 51:33
Dan. 2:35
Hosea 13:3
Micah 4:12
Hab. 3:12

Matt. 3:12
Luke 3:17

Throne

(see also Seat/Throne)

Prayer

Exod. 17:16

Pride

Isa. 14:13

Heaven

Isa. 66:1
Matt. 5:34
Acts 7:49

Jerusalem

Jer. 3:17

Humiliation

Luke 1:52

Restoration

Isa. 52:2

Thunder

God's Judgment

1 Sam. 2:10
1 Sam. 7:10
Isa. 29:6
Amos 1:2
Rev. 4:5
Rev. 8:5
Rev. 10:3–4
Rev. 11:19
Rev. 16:18

God's Power

Job 26:14
Job 36:29
Ps. 77:18
Ps. 93:4
Ps. 104:7
Jer. 10:13
Jer. 51:16
Joel 2:11

God's Voice

2 Sam. 22:14
Job 37:4–5
Job 40:9
Ps. 18:13
Ps. 29:3
Ps. 68:33
Ps. 81:7
Isa. 33:3
Jer. 25:30
Joel 3:16
John 12:29

Impetuous Anger

Mark 3:17

Angelic Voices/Wings

Rev. 6:1
Rev. 9:9
Rev. 14:2
Rev. 19:6

Tongue

Wicked Speech

Job 5:21
Ps. 10:7
Ps. 50:19
Ps. 140:3

Evil Appetite

Job 20:12–13

Discernment

Job 12:11
Job 34:3

Fluency

Ps. 45:1

Deception

Prov. 6:24
Prov. 15:4

Silver

Prov. 10:20

Healing

Prov. 12:18
Prov. 15:4

Honey

Song of Sol. 4:11

Fire

Isa. 30:27
Acts 2:3
James 3:6

Bow

Jer. 9:3

Arrow

Jer. 9:8

Rain

James 1:26

Swords

Ps. 57:4
Ps. 64:3

Vipers

Ps. 140:3

Tooth

(see also Teeth/Fangs)

Unreliability (Bad Tooth)

Prov. 25:19

Torch/Stubs

Enemies

Isa. 7:4

Salvation of Jerusalem

Isa. 62:1

Victorious Leaders

Zech. 12:6

Chariots

Nahum 2:4

Tower/Fortress

God's Name

Prov. 18:10

God

Ps. 61:3

The Bride's Neck/ Nose/Breasts

Song of Sol. 4:4
Song of Sol. 7:4
Song of Sol. 8:10

Trample/Tread (Down)

Forgiveness

Micah 7:19

Victory

Deut. 33:29
2 Sam. 22:43
Ps. 44:5
Ps. 60:12
Ps. 91:13
Ps. 108:13
Isa. 10:6
Isa. 14:25
Isa. 26:6
Isa. 63:2
Micah 7:10
Hab. 3:15
Zech. 10:5
Luke 10:19

Selfish Leaders' Actions

Ezek. 34:18–19
Amos 2:7
Amos 5:11
Amos 8:4

Judgment

Isa. 22:5
Isa. 28:3
Isa. 63:3
Isa. 63:6
Jer. 51:33
Hosea 5:11
Joel 3:13
Mal. 4:3
Rev. 14:20

Sinners Rejecting Truth

Matt. 7:6
Luke 8:5
Heb. 10:29

Conquest

Isa. 63:18
Dan. 7:7
Dan. 7:19
Dan. 7:23
Dan. 8:7
Dan. 8:10
Dan. 8:13
Luke 21:24
Rev. 11:2

Humiliation/Discipline

Isa. 14:19
Isa. 25:10
Lam. 1:15
Lam. 3:16
Matt. 5:13

Generosity

Deut. 25:4
1 Cor. 9:9
1 Tim. 5:18

Irreverent Worship

Isa. 1:12

Traps

Satan's Strategy

1 Tim. 3:7
1 Tim. 6:9
2 Tim. 2:26

Death, Judgment

Job 18:9–10
Luke 21:34

Rash Actions, Words

Prov. 6:2
Prov. 12:13
Prov. 20:15

God

Isa. 8:14

Evil Desires

Prov. 11:6

Godless People

Josh. 23:13

Travail (in Birth)

Divine Judgment

Jer. 4:31
Micah 4:9–10
Matt. 24:8
Mark 13:8
1 Thess. 5:3

Terror

Ps. 48:6
Isa. 13:8
Isa. 21:3
Isa. 26:17–18
Jer. 6:24
Jer. 13:21

Jer. 22:23
Jer. 30:6
Jer. 48:41
Jer. 49:22
Jer. 49:24
Jer. 50:43

Hope

Isa. 54:1
John 16:21–22
Rom. 8:22
Gal. 4:27

A Nation Born (Israel)

Isa. 66:7–8

Nothing Born—Futility

Hos. 13:13

Death

Acts 2:24

Pastoral Concern

Gal. 4:19

Treasure

(see also Lot [Inheritance], Inheritance)

Nation of Israel

Exod. 19:5
Exod. 34:9
Deut. 4:20
Deut. 7:6
Deut. 9:26
Deut. 9:29
Deut. 14:2
Deut. 26:18
Deut. 32:9
1 Sam. 10:1
1 Kings 8:51
1 Kings 8:53
Ps. 28:9
Ps. 33:12
Ps. 74:2
Ps. 78:62
Ps. 78:71
Ps. 79:1
Ps. 94:5
Ps. 94:14
Ps. 106:5
Ps. 106:40
Isa. 19:25
Isa. 63:17
Jer. 10:16
Jer. 12:7–9
Jer. 51:19
Micah 7:18
Zech. 2:12

Death

Job 3:21

Wisdom

Prov. 2:4
Eccles. 7:11
Col. 2:3

God's Blessings

Isa. 33:6
2 Cor. 4:7

God's Kingdom

Matt. 13:44
Matt. 25:34

Reward

Matt. 6:20
Matt. 19:21
Mark 10:21
Luke 12:33–34
Luke 18:22
1 Tim. 6:19

The Nations

Ps. 2:8
Ps. 82:8

God

Lev. 20:24
Deut. 10:9
Josh. 13:33
Ezek. 44:28

Priestly Service

Josh. 18:7

The Saints

Eph. 1:18

Trees

(see also Stump)

God's People

Ps. 1:1
Ps. 52:8
Ps. 92:12
Prov. 11:30
Isa. 1:30
Isa. 61:3
Jer. 11:16
Jer. 17:8
Matt. 12:33

Rulers

Judg. 9:8–15

Wicked People (Judged)

Job 15:33
Job 24:20
Ps. 37:35–36
Ps. 52:5

Hopelessness

Job 19:10

Wisdom

Prov. 3:18

Hope (Fulfilled)

Prov. 13:12

Healing Tongue

Prov. 15:4

Christ

Song of Sol. 2:3

A Lover

Song of Sol. 7:7–8

Judgment

Isa. 10:33
Isa. 17:6
Isa. 24:13
Jer. 46:22
Nahum 3:12
Matt. 3:10
Luke 3:9
Rev. 6:13

Eunuchs

Isa. 56:3

Nations/Kingdoms

Ezek. 17:24
Ezek. 31:1–18
Dan. 4:10–14
Dan. 4:20–26
Hosea 14:6
Hosea 14:8
Zech. 11:1–2
Luke 23:31
Rom. 11:24

Kingdom of Heaven

Matt. 13:32
Luke 13:19

False Teachers

Matt. 7:17–19
Luke 6:43–44
Jude 1:12

God's Servants

Jer. 11:19
Zech. 4:3
Zech. 4:11
Rev. 11:4

Trumpet

Pride

Matt. 6:2

Loudness (Voice)

Isa. 58:1
Rev. 1:10
Rev. 4:1

Dependability

1 Cor. 14:8

Tumbleweed

Judgment

Ps. 83:13
Isa. 17:13

Twigs

Destruction

Hosea 10:7

God's Presence

Isa. 64:1–2

Evidence of Future Events

Matt. 24:32
Mark 13:28

U

Uproot
(see also Plant)

National Discipline
Deut. 28:64
Deut. 29:28
1 Kings 14:15
2 Chron. 7:20
Jer. 12:14–15
Jer. 12:17
Jer. 18:7
Jer. 24:6
Jer. 31:28
Jer. 31:40
Jer. 42:10
Jer. 45:4
Ezek. 17:9
Ezek. 19:12
Dan. 7:8
Dan. 11:4
Amos 9:15
Zeph. 2:4

Judgment of Evil
Ps. 9:6
Ps. 52:5
Prov. 10:30
Prov. 12:3
Jer. 12:17
Micah 5:14

Prophetic Ministry
Jer. 1:10

False Teachers
Jude 1:12

Hope Destroyed
Job 19:10

V

Veil

(see also Mist/Vapor)

Spiritual Blindness

Lam. 3:65
2 Cor. 3:14–15
2 Cor. 4:3

Shame

Isa. 47:2

Prostitute

Gen. 24:65
Song of Sol. 1:7

Venom

Lies

Ps. 58:4
Ps. 140:3

Pagan Corruption

Deut. 32:33

Evil Judged

Job 20:14

Vine

Israel

Ps. 80:8
Ps. 80:14
Ps. 80:16
Isa. 5:1–7
Jer. 2:21
Jer. 6:9
Ezek. 15:1–2
Ezek. 19:10–14

Joseph, Son of Jacob

Gen. 49:22

Sodom and Gomorrah

Deut. 32:32

Wicked People

Job 15:33

Christ

Ezek. 15:3–8
Ezek. 17:1–8
John 15:1–8

Evil World System

Rev. 14:17–20

The Fruitful Wife

Ps. 128:3

Breasts

Song of Sol. 7:8

Vinegar

Undependable Person

Prov. 10:26

Scorn/Persecution

Ps. 69:21
Matt. 27:34
Matt. 27:48
Mark 15:23
Mark 15:36
Luke 23:36
John 19:29

Thoughtlessness, Cruelty

Prov. 25:20

Vomit

Judgment

Lev. 18:25
Lev. 18:28
Lev. 20:22

Personal Consequences for Sin

Job 20:15

People Set Free

Jer. 51:34
Jer. 51:44

Satanic Persecution

Rev. 12:15–16
(See Ps. 124:1–5)

Vultures

Baldness

Micah 1:16

Invading Army

Hab. 1:8

Corruption

Matt. 24:28
Luke 17:37

W

Walking

Fellowship with God

Gen. 5:22
Gen. 5:24
Gen. 6:9
Gen. 17:1
Gen. 24:40
Gen. 48:15
1 Kings 8:25
2 Kings 20:3
2 Chron. 7:17
Ps. 15:2
Ps. 26:3
Ps. 56:13
Ps. 116:9
Isa. 38:3
Isa. 40:31
Isa. 57:2
Micah 6:8
Mal. 2:6
Rom. 4:12
2 Cor. 6:16
1 John 1:7
Rev. 3:4

Obedience

Deut. 5:33
Deut. 8:6
Deut. 10:12
Deut. 19:9
Deut. 26:17
Deut. 28:9
Deut. 30:16
Josh. 22:5
Judg. 2:22
1 Kings 2:3–4
1 Kings 3:3
1 Kings 3:14
1 Kings 8:58
1 Kings 9:4
1 Kings 11:38
2 Chron. 6:16
2 Chron. 6:31
2 Chron. 27:6
Neh. 5:9
Ps. 84:11
Ps. 86:11
Ps. 89:15
Ps. 101:6
Ps. 116:9
Ps. 119:1
Ps. 119:3
Ps. 128:1
Prov. 2:7
Prov. 8:20
Prov. 9:6
Prov. 14:2
Prov. 19:1
Prov. 28:6
Prov. 28:18
Isa. 2:3
Isa. 2:5
Isa. 26:8
Isa. 30:21
Isa. 35:8–9
Isa. 38:15
Isa. 50:10
Jer. 6:16
Jer. 7:23
Hosea 14:9
Micah 4:2
Micah 4:5
Zech. 3:7
Zech. 10:12
John 11:8–10
1 John 2:6
2 John 1:4
2 John 1:6
3 John 1:3–4

Disobedience (Not Walking according to God)

Judg. 2:17
1 Sam. 8:3
1 Sam. 8:5
1 Kings 11:33
2 Kings 21:22
Job 31:5
Ps. 1:1
Prov. 2:13
Prov. 2:20
Prov. 4:14
Isa. 50:11
Isa. 59:8–9
Isa. 65:2
Jer. 6:16
Dan. 4:37
Col. 3:7
1 John 1:6

Danger/Protection

Ps. 23:4

Ps. 142:3
Isa. 43:2

Trouble

Job 29:3
Ps. 138:7

Adultery (Hot Coals)

Prov. 6:28

Defeat

Isa. 51:23

Discipline

Lam. 3:2

Conquest

Ezek. 36:12

God's Care

Prov. 10:9
Prov. 28:26
Isa. 33:15–16
Hosea 11:3

Life

John 8:12

Opportunity

John 12:35

Follow a Bad Example

1 Kings 16:2
1 Kings 16:26
2 Chron. 22:3
2 Chron. 28:2
Ezek. 16:47

Follow a Good Example

2 Kings 22:2
2 Chron. 17:3
2 Chron. 20:32
2 Chron. 34:2

Discouragement

Isa. 9:2

Wall

Salvation

Isa. 26:1
Isa. 60:18

Riches

Prov. 18:11

Lack of Control (Broken Walls)

Prov. 25:28

Army

1 Sam. 25:16

God's Protection

Ezra 9:9

Ability

Ps. 18:29

Weakness/Insecurity

Ps. 62:3

The Bride

Song of Sol. 8:9–10

Sin

Isa. 30:13

God's Servant

Jer. 1:18
Jer. 15:20

Chastening

Lam. 3:7
Lam. 3:9

Protection

Ezek. 22:30

Deceit

Hosea 11:12

Wander

Apostasy

1 Tim. 1:6
1 Tim. 6:10
1 Tim. 6:21
2 Tim. 2:18
James 5:19
2 Peter 2:15

Warfare

(see also Army, Soldier/Warrior)

The Christian Life

1 Cor. 9:7
2 Cor. 10:4
1 Tim. 1:18
1 Tim. 6:12

Battle against Sin

Rom. 7:23
Gal. 5:16–17
James 4:1

Washbasin

Moab (Humiliation)

Ps. 60:8
Ps. 108:9

Washing

Humble Service

John 13:2–17

The Word

Ps. 119:9
Eph. 5:26

Inner Cleansing

Exod. 29:4
Exod. 30:19–21

Exod. 40:12
Ps. 51:2
Ps. 51:7
Isa. 1:16
Isa. 4:4
Jer. 4:14
Heb. 10:22
James 4:8
Rev. 22:14

Innocence

Ps. 26:6
Matt. 27:24

Baptism

Acts 22:16

Watch/Watchman

Swiftness of Time

Ps. 90:4

Prophets

Ezek. 3:17
Ezek. 33:2–7
Hosea 9:8

Leaders

Isa. 56:10
Isa. 62:6

Jer. 6:17

Restoration of Israel

Jer. 31:6

Watchtower

Jerusalem

Micah 4:8

Water (as a Flood)

Personal Trials

Job 22:11
Ps. 69:2
Ps. 69:15
Ps. 88:17
Ps. 124:4

Terror

Job 27:20

Tears

Ps. 6:6
Mal. 2:13

Enemy Invasion

Isa. 8:7
Isa. 59:19
Dan. 9:27
Dan. 11:10
Dan. 11:40

God's Wrath

Isa. 28:2
Hosea 5:10
Nahum 1:8

Sin

1 Peter 4:4

Wealth

Isa. 66:12

Egypt

Jer. 46:8

Water (General References)

Weakness

Ezek. 21:7

Lack of Control

Gen. 49:4

Wickedness

Isa. 57:20

Trouble

Jer. 49:23

Words

Prov. 18:4

A Man's Purposes

Prov. 20:5

Mirror

Prov. 27:19

Insignificance

Isa. 40:15

Water (Spilled/Evaporated/Poured Out)

Groans/Sorrow

Job 3:24
Lam. 2:19

Death

Job 14:11–12
Job 24:18–19
Ps. 22:14
Ps. 79:3

Rain

Job 38:37

Judgment of Wicked

Ps. 58:7

Sacrifice

2 Sam. 23:14–17
1 Chron. 11:16–19

Past Sorrows

Job 11:16

Holy Spirit

Isa. 44:3

Wickedness

Jer. 6:7

Water/Well (for Drinking)

Salvation

Isa. 12:3
Isa. 55:1
Jer. 2:13
John 4:10–14
Rev. 21:6
Rev. 22:17

Turning Trials into Blessings

Ps. 84:6

The Holy Spirit

Exod. 17:5–6
Num. 20:9–11
John 7:37–39
1 Cor. 10:4

Enjoying Evil

Job 15:16
Ps. 109:18
Prov. 9:17

Absence of Shame

Job 34:7

Desire for God

Ps. 42:1
Ps. 63:1

Married Love

Prov. 5:15–16

Adultery

Prov. 9:17

Sinful Leaders

Ezek. 34:18–19

Rejecting God

Jer. 2:13
Jer. 2:18

False Prophets

Jer. 23:15

Good News

Prov. 25:25

Kingdom Blessing

Isa. 35:6
Isa. 41:18
Isa. 41:20
Isa. 44:3
Jer. 31:9

Waves

(see also Floods)

Army

Job 10:17
Jer. 6:23

God's Wrath

Ps. 42:7
Ps. 88:7
Jer. 51:42
Jer. 51:55
Ezek. 26:3
Jonah 2:3

Doubt

James 1:6

Death

2 Sam. 22:5
Ps. 18:4

Nations in Turmoil

Ps. 65:7
Isa. 17:12–13
Ezek. 26:3
Luke 21:25

God's Power

Ps. 89:9
Ps. 93:3
Isa. 48:18
Isa. 51:15
Jer. 31:35
Hab. 3:10

The Wicked

Isa. 57:20

Moral Instability

Gen. 49:4

False Teachers

Jude 1:13

Fear

Ps. 14:5
Ps. 53:5
Ps. 55:5

Guilt

Ps. 38:4

Immaturity

Eph. 4:14

Wax

Weakness

Ps. 22:14

Divine Judgment

Ps. 68:2
Ps. 97:5
Micah 1:4

Weapon

The King

2 Sam. 1:27

Babylon

Jer. 51:20

Wisdom

Eccles. 9:18

Messiah

Isa. 49:2

The Jews

Zech. 9:13

Weaving

(see also Knit/ Weaving)

Swiftness of Life

Job 7:6

Death

Isa. 38:12

Pregnancy

Ps. 139:15

Weeds

Lawsuits

Hosea 10:4

Counterfeit Christians

Matt. 13:25–30
Matt. 13:36–41

Weighing

Judging (Actions, Motives)

1 Sam. 2:3
Job 31:6
Prov. 16:2
Prov. 21:2
Prov. 24:12
Dan. 5:27

Burden of Sin

Ezek. 33:10
Luke 21:34

Discerning Truth

Prov. 15:28
1 Cor. 14:29

Misery

Job 6:2–3

Burden of Age

Jer. 6:11

Burden of Anxiety

Job 6:2
Prov. 12:25
Eccles. 6:1
Eccles. 8:6

Value

Lam. 4:2
John 5:36

Discipline

Lam. 3:7

Glory

2 Cor. 4:17

Wheels

God's Providence

Ezek. 1:15–21
Ezek. 10:2–19
Ezek. 11:22
Dan. 7:9

Death

Eccles. 12:6

Whirlwind

(see also Storms, Wind/Whirlwind)

Judgment

Prov. 1:27
Isa. 40:24
Jer. 23:19
Hosea 4:19
Hosea 8:7
Nahum 1:3
Zech. 7:14

Speed

Isa. 5:28
Isa. 66:15
Jer. 4:13

Whitewash

Hypocrisy, Cover-Up

Ezek. 13:1–16
Ezek. 22:28–30
Matt. 23:27
Acts 23:3

Wick

God's Enemies

Isa. 42:3
Isa. 43:17
Matt. 12:20

Widow

Desertion

Lam. 1:1

Arrogance

Isa. 47:8–9
Rev. 18:7

Wife

(see also Bride)

The Church

Eph. 5:22
Rev. 21:9

Israel (Adulterous Wife)

Jer. 2:1
Ezek. 16:32
Hosea 1:2
Hosea 3:1

Images of the Faithful Wife

Fruitful Vine

Ps. 128:3

Crown

Prov. 12:4

Images of the Unfaithful Wife

Decay

Prov. 12:4

Narrow Well

Prov. 23:27

Image of the Nagging Wife

Dripping

Prov. 19:13
Prov. 27:15

Win

Make Converts

Prov. 11:30
Matt. 23:15
Acts 14:21
1 Cor. 9:19–22
Gal. 4:17
1 Peter 3:1

Be Rewarded

Phil. 3:14

Reconciliation

Matt 18:15

Wind/Whirlwind

(see also Breath, Storms)

God's Messengers

2 Sam. 22:11
Ps. 11:6
Ps. 18:10
Ps. 18:15
Ps. 104:3–4
Ps. 148:8
Heb. 1:7

God's Judgment

Exod. 15:10
Job 21:18
Job 30:15
Ps. 1:4
Ps. 11:6
Ps. 18:15
Ps. 35:5
Ps. 68:2
Ps. 83:13
Prov. 1:27
Isa. 11:15
Isa. 17:13
Isa. 24:20
Isa. 28:2
Isa. 41:16
Isa. 57:13
Isa. 64:6
Jer. 4:11
Jer. 13:24
Jer. 18:17
Jer. 22:22
Jer. 30:23
Ezek. 1:4
Ezek. 13:11
Ezek. 13:13
Ezek. 17:10
Ezek. 19:12
Ezek. 27:26
Dan. 2:35
Hosea 4:19
Hosea 8:7
Hosea 13:15

Words

Job 6:26
Job 8:1–2
Job 15:2
Prov. 25:14
Jer. 5:13

Vanity, Futility of Life

Prov. 11:29
Eccles. 1:14
Eccles. 1:17
Eccles. 2:11
Eccles. 2:17
Eccles. 2:26
Eccles. 4:4
Eccles. 4:6
Eccles. 4:16
Eccles. 5:16
Eccles. 6:9
Eccles. 8:8
Isa. 26:18
Isa. 41:29
Hosea 8:7
Hosea 12:1

Quarrelsome Person

Prov. 27:16

Man's Weakness

Job 13:25
Prov. 30:4

Idols

Isa. 41:29

Sin

Isa. 64:6

Invasion

Isa. 41:2
Jer. 4:11–12
Hab. 1:9
Hab. 1:11

Compromise

Matt. 11:7
Luke 7:24

Image of Spirit of God

Ezek. 37:4–10
John 3:8
Acts 2:2

False Doctrine

Eph. 4:14

God's Creative Power

Job 37:10
Ps. 33:6
Ezek. 17:1–14

False Prophets

Jer. 5:13

Window

Blindness

Eccles. 12:3

Opportunity

2 Kings 13:17

Judgment

Hosea 13:3

Wine/Wine Press

(see also Drunk/ Drunkenness)

Prosperity

Gen. 27:28
Gen. 27:37
Gen. 49:11
Deut. 33:28
2 Kings 18:32
Prov. 3:10
Isa. 36:17
Hosea 14:7
Joel 3:18
Amos 9:13

Divine Wrath

Ps. 75:8
Isa. 49:26
Isa. 51:17
Isa. 51:21–22
Isa. 63:2–3
Isa. 63:6
Jer. 25:15
Jer. 25:17
Jer. 25:28
Jer. 49:12
Lam. 1:15
Zech. 9:16
Rev. 14:10
Rev. 14:19–20
Rev. 16:19
Rev. 19:15

Corruption/ Compromise

Deut. 32:32–33
Jer. 51:7
Rev. 14:8
Rev. 17:2
Rev. 18:3

Inner Compulsion

Job 32:19
Jer. 23:9

Affliction

Ps. 60:3

Joy

Ps. 4:7
Ps. 104:15

Love

Song of Sol. 1:2
Song of Sol. 1:4
Song of Sol. 4:10
Song of Sol. 7:9

Cheapening/Decay

Isa. 1:22

Kingdom Blessings

Isa. 25:6
Isa. 55:1
Matt. 9:17
Mark 2:22
Luke 5:37

Complacency

Jer. 48:11
Zeph. 1:12

Wings

(see also Shadows/ Shade)

Security (Holy of Holies or Hen's Wings)

Ruth 2:12
Ps. 36:7
Ps. 57:1
Ps. 61:4
Ps. 63:7
Ps. 91:4

Matt. 23:37
Luke 13:34

Deliverance

Exod. 19:4
2 Sam. 22:11
Isa. 40:31
Rev. 12:14

Protection

Deut. 32:10–11
Ps. 17:8

Escape

Ps. 55:6

Dawn

Ps. 139:9
Mal. 4:2

Wind

2 Sam. 22:11
Ps. 18:10
Ps. 104:3

Vanity of Wealth

Prov. 23:5

Invasion

Jer. 48:40
Jer. 49:22
Ezek. 17:3
Ezek. 17:7
Dan. 7:4
Dan. 7:6

Surrender

Isa. 10:14

Winnowing

(see also Sieve/Sift/ Winnow)

Israel's Victory

Isa. 41:16

Judgment

Jer. 15:7
Jer. 51:2
Matt. 3:12
Luke 3:17

A King's Justice

Prov. 20:8
Prov. 20:26

Wiping

Judgment

Gen. 6:7
Gen. 7:4
Gen. 7:23
Exod. 9:15
Exod. 23:23
Exod. 32:12
Josh. 9:24
Judg. 21:17
1 Sam. 15:18
2 Kings 21:13
Zeph. 1:11

Opposition

Ps. 119:87

Forgiveness

Acts 3:19

Comfort

Isa. 25:8
Rev. 7:17
Rev. 21:4

Unforgiveness

Prov. 6:33

Wolf/Wolves

Tribe of Benjamin

Gen. 49:27

Peace/Harmony

Isa. 11:6
Isa. 65:25

Enemies (Invasion)

Jer. 5:6
Hab. 1:8
Matt. 10:16
Luke 10:3
John 10:12
Acts 20:29

Evil Leaders

Ezek. 22:27
Zeph. 3:3
Acts 20:29

False Prophets/ Hypocrites

Matt. 7:15

Fierceness

Gen. 49:27
Hab. 1:8

Woman/Women

Weakness

Nahum 3:13

Disgrace

Judg. 4:9
Judg. 9:53–54
2 Sam. 11:21

Pain, Judgment (Labor)

Ps. 48:6
Isa. 13:8
Isa. 21:3
Isa. 26:17
Isa. 42:14
Jer. 6:4
Jer. 13:21
Jer. 22:23

Jer. 30:6
Jer. 48:41
Jer. 49:22
Jer. 49:24
Jer. 50:43
Hosea 13:13
Micah 4:9–10
1 Thess. 5:3

Idolatry (Unfaithfulness)

Jer. 3:20

Wickedness

Zech. 5:7–8

Babylon

Rev. 17:3–9

Israel

Rev. 12:1
Rev. 12:6
Rev. 12:13–17

Womb
(see also Birth)

Dawn (Day Is Born)

Ps. 110:3

Planning Sin

Job 15:35
James 1:15

Creation

Job 38:8

Wood

Gossip

Prov. 26:20–21

Sinners

Jer. 5:14
Ezek. 15:6–7
Ezek. 19:10–14
Ezek. 20:46–48
Ezek. 21:32
Ezek. 30:8
Ezek. 30:14
Ezek. 30:16
Ezek. 39:6
Matt. 3:10–12

Salvation

Amos 4:11
Zech. 3:2
Jude 1:23

Unworthy Ministry

1 Cor. 3:12

Conquerors

Zech. 12:6

Wool

Snow

Ps. 147:16

Cleansing/ Whiteness/The Eternal

Isa. 1:18
Dan. 7:9
Rev. 1:14

Judgment

Isa. 51:8

Worm/Maggot

Man

Job 25:6

Jesus

Ps. 22:6

Death

Job 17:14
Job 21:26
Job 24:20
Isa. 14:11
Isa. 51:8

Israel

Isa. 41:14

Punishment

Isa. 66:24
Mark 9:48

False Teachers

2 Tim. 3:6

Wounds
(see also Bruises/ Wounds)

Personal Burdens

Ps. 109:22
Jer. 10:19
Jer. 15:18

National Sin

Isa. 1:6
Jer. 6:7
Jer. 6:14
Jer. 8:11
Jer. 8:22
Jer. 30:12
Jer. 30:15
Lam. 2:13
Micah 1:9

Punishment/ Chastening

Deut. 32:39
Jer. 14:17
Jer. 19:8
Jer. 49:17
Jer. 50:13
Lam. 2:13
Nahum 3:19

God's Loving Care/ Forgiveness

Job 5:18
Ps. 147:3
Isa. 30:26
Jer. 30:17
Hosea 6:1

Friendly Counsel

Prov. 27:6

Forgiveness

Isa. 53:5
1 Peter 2:24

Wreath

City of Samaria

Isa. 28:1
Isa. 28:3

God

Isa. 28:5

Wrestle

Internal Conflict

Ps. 13:2

Prayer

Col. 4:12

Y

Yeast

False Teaching

Matt. 16:6
Matt. 16:11–12
Mark 8:15
Luke 12:1
Gal. 5:9

Kingdom of Heaven

Matt. 13:33
Luke 13:20–21

The Old Life

1 Cor. 5:6–8

Hypocrisy

Luke 12:1

Yoke

Bondage (Political, Spiritual)

Deut. 28:48
1 Kings 12:4
1 Kings 12:9–14
2 Chron. 10:4
2 Chron. 10:9–14
Isa. 47:6
Jer. 27:2
Jer. 27:8
Jer. 27:11–12
Lam. 1:14
Acts 15:10
Gal. 5:1
1 Tim. 6:1

Rebellion (Take Off Yoke)

Jer. 5:5

Show Mercy (Remove Yoke)

Isa. 58:6
Isa. 58:9

Freedom (Break Yoke)

Gen. 27:40
Exod. 6:6–7
Lev. 26:13
Isa. 9:4
Isa. 10:27
Isa. 14:25
Jer. 2:20
Jer. 28:2
Jer. 28:4
Jer. 28:10–14
Jer. 30:8
Ezek. 30:18
Ezek. 34:27
Hosea 11:4
Nahum 1:13

Discipline

Lam. 3:27
Hosea 10:11

Submission to Christ

Matt. 11:29–30

Compromise with Sin

Num. 25:3
Num. 25:5
Ps. 106:28
2 Cor. 6:14

Workers Together

Phil. 4:3

Warren W. Wiersbe is Distinguished Professor of Preaching at Grand Rapids Baptist Seminary and has pastored churches in Indiana, Kentucky, and Illinois (Chicago's historic Moody Memorial). He is the author and editor of more than one hundred books and now focuses his energies on writing, teaching, and conference ministry.